Mackey's National Freemason.

Vol. I. OCTOBER, 1871. No. 1.

SALUTATORY.

BY THE EDITOR.

In assuming, at the capital of the nation, the editorship of a new Masonic periodical, we cannot refrain from expressing the gratification we experience at the prospect of a renewal of literary intercourse with our brethren—an intercourse which, in by-gone years, was so pleasant to ourselves, and, we would fain hope, not wholly uninteresting to our readers.

There is some difference between the author of a book and the editor of a magazine, in the reciprocal relations which exist between each one and his readers—a relation which very forcibly suggests itself to our mind at this time. The author of a book, however valuable or important its contents, comes to his readers like the visitor who bears a letter of intro-duction. He is received with hospitable attention, a friendly grasp of the hand, and a pleasant conversation; but after a time the visitor is dis-missed, or the book laid on the shelf, to be seen, and, perhaps, to be thought of no more, or the former may be met at some future period with a brief but courteous salutation, or the latter taken up for a casual reference. But the relations of an editor of a magazine with his patrons are like those of two friendly and familiar neighbors: long-continued in-tercourse gives to each an interest in the other, and the visits, monthly repeated, are looked for with fond anticipations. The number for Jan-uary is laid down with regret, and the one for February is looked for with anxiety. The editor and his readers, if the work is well conducted, and gives the satisfaction which every honest editor strives to bestow, are apt to exclaim, in the language of the old Masonic formula, on the issue of every number, "Happy to meet, sorry to part, happy to meet again."

Such is the relation which we, as the editor of "MACKEY'S NATIONAL FREEMASON," are desirous of cultivating between that work and its patrons. For that purpose we promise to devote all our energies and all our abil-ities to the production of a work of which each successive number shall contain matters interesting and instructive to the Craft. It has been said, and perhaps with truth, that he who is good at making promises is seldom good for anything else; and there is an old French proverb, which sneers at him who promises "mountains and marvels;" but some promise must be made, that there may be a basis for expectation, and we will at least conscientiously strive not to

"Keep the word of promise to the ear, and break it to the hope."

Our first effort will be to make the NATIONAL FREEMASON a magazine of high Masonic standing. For this purpose no articles will be admitted into its pages of a trifling or worthless character; nothing that will not be productive of interest or instruction to its readers. And while it is intended, by our own personal labors and the contributions of many prominent Masons, whose valued assistance has been engaged, to secure permanently this elevated tone to the magazine, other resources of every kind will be appealed to, to make its pages a repository of Masonic intelligence; nor shall its contents be of such a nature as to render it uncongenial to the tastes of the numerous readers whom it will seek to win. It will be learned without being abstruse, instructive without being tedious; so that all, however diversified may be their intellectual tastes or acquirements, may find something in it to interest them, and make them wish for a renewal of its visits. It is needless to expatiate on the general plan, which has been explained in the prospectus. It is sufficient to say, that all that has been there promised will, so far as human strength prevails, be faithfully executed.

In the very outset of the renewal of an editorial intercourse with the Fraternity, it is but just and proper that we should honestly state the position that we take, and the sentiments that we hold, on the much-debated question of Masonic publications. Many well-meaning but timid members of the Fraternity object to the freedom with which Masonic topics are discussed in printed works. They think that the veil is too much withdrawn by modern Masonic writers, and that all doctrine and insruction should be confined to oral teaching, within the limits of the Lodge-room. Hence, to them the art of printing becomes useless for the diffusion of Masonic knowledge, and thus, whatever may be the attainments of a Masonic scholar, the fruits of his study and experience would be confined to the narrow limits of his personal presence. Such objectors draw no distinction between the ritual and the philosophy of Masonry. Like the old priests of Egypt, they would have everything concealed under hieroglyphics, and would as soon think of opening a Lodge in public as they would of discussing, in a printed book, the principles and design of the Institution.

Fourteen years ago the committee of foreign correspondence of a prominent Grand Lodge could affirm without, as they supposed, "danger of contradiction," that Masonic literature was "doing more harm than good to the Institution." About the same time the committee of another equally prominent Grand Lodge were not ashamed to express their regret that so much prominence of notice is, "in several Grand Lodge proceedings, given to Masonic publications. Masonry existed and flourished, was harmonious and happy, in their absence."

When we read such diatribes against Masonic literature and Masonic progress—such blind efforts to hide under the bushel the light that should be on the hill-top—we are incontinently reminded of a similar iconoclast, who, more than four centuries ago, made a like onslaught on the pernicious effects of learning.

The immortal Jack Cade, in condemning Lord Say to death as a patron of learning, gave vent to words of which the language of these enemies of Masonic literature seems to be but the echo:

"Thou hast most traitorously corrupted the youth of the realm, in erecting a grammar school; and whereas, before, our forefathers had no other books but the score and the tally, thou hast caused printing to be used; and, contrary to the king, his crown, and dignity, thou hast built a paper-mill. It will be proved to thy face that thou hast men about thee that usually talk of a noun and a verb, and such abominable words as no Christian ear can endure to hear."

We belong to no such school. On the contrary, we believe that too much cannot be written and printed and read about the philosophy and history, the science and symbolism, of Freemasonry: provided always the writing is confided to those who rightly understand their art. In Masonry, as in astronomy, in geology, or in any other of the arts and sciences, a new book by an expert must always be esteemed a valuable contribution. The productions of silly and untutored minds will fall of themselves into oblivion without the aid of official persecution; but that which is really valuable—which presents new facts, or furnishes suggestive thoughts—will, in spite of the denunciations of the Jack Cades of Masonry, live to instruct the brethren, and to elevate the tone and standing of the Institution.

Rather would we enlist under the banner of the venerable Oliver, who has said on this subject:

"I conceive it to be an error in judgment to discountenance the publication of philosophical disquisitions on the subject of Freemasonry, because such a proceeding would not only induce the world to think that our pretensions are incapable of enduring the test of inquiry, but would also have a tendency to restore the dark ages of superstition, when even the sacred writings were prohibited, under an apprehension that their contents might be misunderstood or perverted to the propagation of unsound doctrines and pernicious practices; and thus would ignorance be transmitted, as a legacy, from one generation to another."

Years ago, we uttered on this subject sentiments which we now take occasion to repeat:

" Without an adequate course of reading, no Mason can now take a position of any distinction in the ranks of the Fraternity. Without extending his studies beyond what is taught in the brief lectures of the Lodge, he can never properly appreciate the end and nature of Freemasonry as a speculative science. The lectures constitute but the skeleton of Masonic science. The muscles and nerves and blood vessels, which are to give vitality, and beauty, and health, and vigor to that lifeless skeleton, must be found in the commentaries on them which the learning and research of Masonic writers have given to the Masonic student."

It is fifteen years since these words were first uttered, and fifteen years of enlarged experience have furnished us with no reasons for a change of our convictions. On this platform, then, we stand, and on these principles we shall conduct the NATIONAL FREEMASON. Abstaining, with due caution, from any unnecessary reference to that which it is forbidden to communicate, leaving the ritual and the aporheta or esoteric doctrines under the vail which the obligations of Masonry have thrown around them, we shall indulge with great, but, we trust, with judicious latitude, in the discussion and investigation of the traditions and the symbolism, the history and the jurisprudence, the philosophy and the science, of the Order; and in this course we confidently believe that we will be sustained by every intelligent member of the fraternity.

The editor—not now making his " first appearance on the boards," but rather, like an old actor, who has long since lost his " stage fright"—comes before the public with but little timidity, but rather with the confidence that he is among old friends, who will give to him in this undertaking, as they have done in the long past of his Masonic life, their unalterable kindness and continued good will.

GENIUS.—Prince Puckler-Muskau visited Rothschild while in London. He found that he spoke "in a language peculiar to himself—half German, the English part with a broad German accent." This sort of language struck the prince as being very characteristic of a person of genius.

The corollary from all this is, that to speak broken English is a mark of genius—in a millionaire; but in a beggar—of course not.

PARLIAMENTARY LAW, AS APPLIED TO THE GOVERNMENT OF MASONIC BODIES.

BY ALBERT G. MACKEY, M. D.

CHAPTER I.

PRELIMINARY.

Parliamentary Law, or the *Lex Parliamentaria*, is that code originally framed for the government of the Parliament of Great Britain in the transaction of its business, and subsequently adopted, with necessary modifications, by the Congress of the United States.

It must not be supposed, from the name, that no such law was known before the establishment of the British Parliament. It is evident that at all times when, and in all countries where, deliberative bodies have existed, it must have been found necessary to establish some regulations by which business might be facilitated. The parliamentary law of England and America has been reduced by long experience to the accuracy of a science, but it is not to be supposed that other, though simpler, systems did not prevail in former times. In the Roman Senate, for instance, although, judging from the character of such productions as Cicero's Orations against Catiline and his Philippics against Antony, rules of order could not have been rigidly enforced; yet we know from historic evidence, that the proceedings of that body were regulated by an established system of rules. The parliamentary law of Rome was not so extensive as that of England or America, but it was just as positive, for all the purposes which it was intended to accomplish. Thus, the times and places of meeting and adjournment of the Senate, the qualifications of its members, the number that constituted a quorum, and the mode and manner of taking the question or of proposing and perfecting a law, were all absolutely defined by statutory regulations; the intention of which was, to secure a faithful and orderly transaction of public business. A similar system prevailed in all the other countries of antiquity, where deliberative bodies existed.

But what was found requisite for the regulation of public bodies, that order might be secured and the rights of all be respected, has been found equally necessary in private societies. Indeed, no association of men could meet together for the discussion of any subject, with the slightest probability of ever coming to a conclusion, unless its debates were regulated by certain and acknowledged rules.

The rules thus adopted for its government are called its parliamentary law, and they are selected from the parliamentary law of the national assembly, because that code has been instituted by the wisdom of past ages, and modified and perfected by the experience of subsequent ones, so that it is now universally acknowledged, that there is no better system of government for deliberative societies than the code which has so long been in operation under the name of Parliamentary Law.

Of course, as these private societies are restrained within inferior limits, exercise less extensive powers, and differ in their organizations and in the objects of their association, many portions of the Parliamentary Law, which are necessary in the business of Parliament or Congress, must be inapplicable to them. But, so far as their peculiar character requires, the Parliamentary Law has been adopted for the government of these societies.

Seeing, then, how necessary it is that every association, convened for deliberative purposes, should have specific rules for its government, and seeing also that just such a code of rules, the results of the sagacity of wise men, and well tried by the experience of several centuries, is to be found in the Parliamentary Law, it is surprising that any one should be found who would object to the application of this law to the government of Masonic bodies; and yet there are Masons who really believe that the government of a Lodge or Chapter by parliamentary law would be an infringement on the ancient landmarks, and a violation of the spirit of the Institution. And these men, too, at the very time of their objecting, are benefiting by the lights and following the directions of this very law, to which they appear to be so inimical; for no presiding officer can recognize a speaker, put a question, or decide the results of a division, without referring for the manner in which these duties are performed to the usages of parliamentary law.

There are, it is true, on the other hand, some Masons, not well instructed in the jurisprudence of the Order, and not conversant with the peculiarities of the organization, in which it differs from other associations, who would apply to it indiscriminately the rules of parliamentary law, and thus would decide many questions contrary to the spirit of the Institution. Both of these are wrong. There is a *mezzo termino,* or neutral ground, on which it is wisest to rest. Here, as elsewhere, a middle course will be found the safest: *Medio tutissimus ibis*—we shall consult truth and propriety by avoiding all extremes.

The true state of the case is this: Masonry has an organization peculiar to itself. Wherever this organization comes in conflict with that of other associations, the parliamentary law will be inapplicable. Where, on the contrary, this organization does not differ in a Lodge from that of other deliberative bodies, the rules of order by which such a Lodge should be governed will be best found in the provisions of the Parliamentary Law. Let us illustrate this by examples.

Under the operation of the unwritten laws of Masonry a Lodge cannot adjourn, but must be closed by the Worshipful Master at his good will and pleasure. Now, in the Parliamentary Law there are provisions for the government of adjournments, such, for instance, as that a motion to that effect must take precedence of all other motions. This rule is applicable to all societies, wherein the members have reserved to themselves the right of adjournment ; but is wholly inadmissible in a Masonic Lodge, where no such right exists. If, then, such a motion for adjournment should be made in a Lodge, it would not be necessary that the presiding officer should refer for his instructions to the provisions of parliamentary law in reference to adjournment. He would at once declare the proceeding out of order, and would properly refuse to entertain the motion.

Again, although the members of a Lodge cannot select the time of adjournment, they have an undoubted right to close at any time a debate, in which the Lodge may be engaged, when they deem it improper or inexpedient to continue the discussion. Now, there are various modes of closing a debate, all of which are defined and regulated by parliamentary law. One of these is by a call for the previous question. Although there is no positive law on the subject, yet the spirit of comity and courtesy which prevails in the Institution, the authority of the best Masonic jurists, and the general usage of the Fraternity, have concurred in the decision, that the previous question cannot be moved in a Masonic Lodge. All the provisions, therefore, of the Parliamentary Law, which refer to the subject of the previous question, are inapplicable in Masonry, and need not be studied by the Master of a Lodge.

But the other methods of closing a debate are not in this category. These methods are, to postpone to a time certain, to postpone indefinitely, and to lie upon the table. Each of these methods must be inaugurated by a motion to that effect, and these motions are regulated by parliamentary law, having each an order of priority and preference, and two of them being debatable as to the expediency of adoption, while the third admits of no discussion, but must be put to the assembly immediately after it is made. In all of these cases, it is necessary that the presiding officer should be conversant with the parliamentary law in the premises, if he would avoid confusion and facilitate the dispatch of business.

Not only, then, is a thorough knowledge of parliamentary law necessary for the presiding officer of a Masonic body, if he would discharge the duties of the chair with credit to himself and comfort to the members, but he must be possessed of the additional information as to what parts of that law are applicable to Masonry, and what parts are not; as to where and when he must refer to it for the decision of a question, and where and when he must lay it aside, and rely for his government upon the organic law and the ancient usages of the Institution.

A treatise, then, which should accurately define the parliamentary law in its application to the government of Masonic bodies, showing precisely the points in which it must be pursued and those in which it must be abandoned—which should indicate the alternating prominence of the parliamentary law and the organic law of Masonry, and which should thus present the presiding officer with a chart, pointing out the intricate channels and hidden rocks and under-currents which render every discussion in a deliberative body liable to confusion, which give rise to turbulence, which needlessly protract business, and make doubtful the success of truth—cannot be unacceptable or unprofitable as a contribution to the jurisprudence of the Order.

I propose, then, in several succeeding chapters, to undertake such a task. Defining, accurately, the prerogatives of the chair and the privileges of the members, and the difference between the *business* and the *work* of a Lodge—terms of great significance, and which have an important bearing upon the relations of the parliamentary law and the law of Masonry— I shall proceed to lay down the rules and regulations by which the Master of a Lodge may be enabled to conduct the business of the body over which he has been called to preside according to those well-settled principles of government by which alone confusion can be arrested and order preserved.

Although the term Master of a Lodge is used for the sake of brevity of expression, and to avoid a needless augmentation of words, it must be understood that the remarks made in reference to that officer are equally applicable to the presiding officer of higher bodies, such as Chapters, Councils, and Commanderies, unless the character of the remark itself, or a specific notice made at the time, should indicate that the principle laid down is to be restricted to symbolic Masonry.

But it must not be inferred that what is said of the government of subordinate Lodges or Chapters, Councils or Commanderies, is equally applicable to the Grand Bodies in those respective divisions of the Rite. A Grand Lodge, for instance, has a different organization from that of its subordinates. The prerogatives of a Grand Master are more extensive than those of a Master; and the privileges of the representatives who make up the governing body are necessarily superior to those which inure to the members of their subordinate bodies. Hence there is some discrimination to be observed in the application of the parliamentary law to the government of Grand Lodges, Grand Chapters, Grand Councils, and Grand Commanderies. These will therefore be, on appropriate occasions, specifically referred to, as well as made in distinct chapters the special subjects of investigation.

In the next chapter I shall enter, as a preliminary labor, into an inquiry as to what are the prerogatives of the Master of a Lodge, and as to what are the privileges of its members; an inquiry which will necessarily include a discussion of that important and interesting question: What is the difference between the *work* and the *business* of a Lodge? This, indeed, will be found to be, as we go on, a key for the solution of almost all the different problems of Masonic parliamentary law.

THE STONEMASONS OF THE MIDDLE AGES, THE PRECURSORS OF THE FREEMASONS.

An Historical Sketch, in Two Chapters.

BY ALBERT G. MACKEY, M. D.

CHAPTER I.

FROM CHARLEMAGNE TO THE CATHEDRAL OF STRASBURG.

The history of the origin and progress of the Brotherhood of Stonemasons in Europe, during the Middle Ages, is of great importance, as a study, to the Masonic scholar, because of the intimate connection that existed between that Brotherhood and the Fraternity of Freemasons. Indeed, the history of the one is but the introduction to the history of the other. In an historical excursus, we are compelled to take up the speculative science where we find it left by the operative art. Hence, whoever shall undertake to write a history of Freemasonry, must give, for the completion of his labor, a very full consideration to the Brotherhood of Stonemasons.

In the year 1820, there issued from the press of Leipsic, in Germany, a work, by Dr. Christian Ludwig Steiglitz, under the title of *Von Altdeutscher Baukunst*, that is, "An Essay on the Old German Architecture." In this work the author traces, with great exactness, the rise and the progress of the fraternities of Stonemasons from the earliest times, through the Middle Ages, until their final absorption into the associations of Freemasons. From the labors of Dr. Steiglitz, collated with some other authorities in respect to matters upon which he is either silent or erroneous, I have compiled the following sketch.

It is universally admitted that, in the early ages of Christianity, the clergy alone were the patrons of the arts and sciences. This was because all learning was then almost exclusively confined to ecclesiastics. Very few of the laity could read or write, and even kings affixed the sign of the cross, in the place of their signatures, to the charters and other documents which they issued, because, as they frankly confessed, of their inability to write their names; and hence comes the modern expression of *signing* a paper, as equivalent to subscribing the name.

From the time of Charlemagne, in the eighth century, to the middle of the twelfth, all knowledge and practice of architecture, painting, and sculpture were exclusively confined to the monks; and bishops personally superintended the erection of the churches and cathedrals in their dioceses, because not only the principles, but the practice of the art of building were secrets scrupulously maintained within the walls of cloisters, and utterly unknown to laymen.

Many of the founders of the Monastic Orders, and especially among these St. Benedict, made it a peculiar duty for the brethren to devote themselves to architecture and church building. The English monk Winfrid, better known in ecclesiastical history as St. Boniface, and who, for his labors in Christianizing that country, has been styled the Apostle of Germany, followed the example of his predecessors in the erection of German monasteries. In the eighth century he organized an especial class of monks for the practice of building, under the names of *Operarii*, or Craftsmen, and *Magistri Operum*, or Masters of the Works. The labors and duties of these monks were divided. Some of them designed the plan of the building; others were painters and sculptors; others were occupied in working in gold and silver and embroidery; and others again, who were called *Cæmentarii*, or Stonemasons, undertook the practical labors of construction. Sometimes, especially in extensive buildings, where many workmen were required, laymen were also employed, under the direction of the monks. So extensive did these labors become, that bishops and abbots often derived a large portion of their revenues from the earnings of the workmen in the monasteries.

Among the laymen, who were employed in the monasteries, as assistants and laborers, many were of course possessed of superior intelligence. The constant and intimate association of these with the monks in the prosecution of the same design led to this result, that in process of time, gradually and almost unconsciously, the monks imparted to them their art secrets and the esoteric principles of architecture. Then, by degrees, the knowledge of the arts and sciences went from these monkish builders out into the world, and the laymen architects, withdrawing from the ecclesiastical fraternities, organized brotherhoods of their own. Such was the beginning of the Masonic fraternities in Germany, and the same thing occurred in other countries. These brotherhoods of Masons now began to be called upon, as the monks formerly had been, when an important building, and especially a church or a cathedral, was to be erected. Eventually they entirely superseded their monkish teachers in the prosecution of the art of building. To their knowledge of architecture they added that of the other sciences, which they had learned from the monks. Like these, too, they devoted themselves to the higher principles of the art, and employed other laymen to assist their labors as stonemasons. And thus the union of these architects and stonemasons presented, in the midst of an uneducated people, a more elevated and intelligent class, engaged as an exclusive association in building important and especially religious edifices.

But now a new classification took place. As formerly, the monks, who were the sole depositaries of the secrets of high art, separated themselves from the laymen, who were intrusted with only the manual labor of building; so now the more intelligent of the laymen, who had received these secrets from the monks, were distinguished as architects from the ordinary laborers or common masons. The latter knew only the use of the trowel and mortar, while the former were occupied in devising plans for building and in the construction of ornaments by sculpture and skillful stonecutting.

These brotherhoods of high artists soon won great esteem, and many privileges and franchises were conceded to them by the municipal authorities among whom they practiced their profession. Their places of assembly were called *Hutten, Logen,* or *Lodges,* and the members took the name of *Freemasons.* Their patron saint was St. John the Baptist, who was honored by them as the mediator between the old and the new covenants, and the first martyr of the Christian religion. To what condition of art these Freemasons of the Middle Ages had attained, we may judge from what Hallam says of the edifices they erected—that they "united sublimity in general composition with the beauties of variety and form, skillful or at least fortunate effects of shadow and light, and in some instances extraordinary mechanical science." (*Mid. Ages,* iv, 280.) And he subsequently adds, as an involuntary confirmation of the truth of the sketch of their origin just given, that the mechanical execution of the buildings was "so far beyond the apparent intellectual powers of those times, that some have ascribed the principal ecclesiastical structures to the Fraternity of Freemasons, depositaries of a concealed and traditionary science. There is probably some ground for this opinion, and the earlier archives of that mysterious association, if they existed, might illustrate the progress of Gothic architecture, and perhaps reveal its origin." (*Ib.,* 284.) These archives do exist, or many of them; and although unknown to Mr. Hallam, because they were out of the course of his usual reading, they have been thoroughly sifted by recent Masonic scholars, especially by our German and English brethren; and that which the historian of the Middle Ages had only assumed as a plausible conjecture has, by their researches, been proved to be a fact.

The prevalence of gnostic symbols—such as lions, serpents, and the like—in the decorations of the churches of the Middle Ages, have led some writers to conclude, that the Knights Templars exercised an influence over the architects, and that by them the Gnostic and ophite symbols were introduced into Europe.   But Dr. Steiglitz denies the correctness of this conclusion.   He ascribes the existence of Gnostic symbols in the church architecture to the fact that, at an early period in ecclesiastical history, many of the Gnostic dogmas passed over into Christendom with the Oriental and Platonic philosophy, and he attributes their adoption in architecture to the natural compliance of the architects or Freemasons with the predominant taste in the earlier periods of the Middle Ages for mysticism, and the favor given to grotesque decorations, which were admired without any knowledge of their actual import.

That there ever was any association of the Knights Templars with the Freemasons is still an uncertain and an undetermined point of history. If it did take place, it must have been at a very late period; and if any community or similarity of symbolism is to be detected among the two Orders, it is more reasonable to ascribe it to the circumstance, that the Templars always associated a body of architects with themselves for the erection of their own churches and other buildings, and that these architects were united in one and the same fraternity with the Freemasons, whose secrets they possessed and whose architectural opinions they shared.

Steiglitz also denies any deduction of the Builders' Fraternities, or Masonic Lodges, of the Middle Ages, from the Mysteries of the old Indians, Egyptians, and Greeks, although he acknowledges that there is a resemblance between the organizations.   This, however, he attributes to the fact, that the Indians and Egyptians preserved all the sciences, as well as the principles of architecture, among their secrets, and because, among the Greeks, the artists were initiated into their mysteries, so that, in the old as well as in the new brotherhoods, there was a purer knowledge of religious truth, which elevated them as distinct associations above the people.   In like manner, he denies the descent of the Masonic fraternities from the sect of Pythagoreans, which they resembled only in this: that the Samian sage established schools which were secret, and were based upon the principles of geometry.

But he thinks that those are not mistaken who trace the associations of Masons of the Middle Ages to the Roman Colleges, the *Collegia*

Cæmentariorum, because these colleges appear in every country that was conquered and established as a province or a colony by the Romans, where they erected temples and other public buildings, and promoted the civilization of the inhabitants. They continued until a late period. But when Rome began to be convulsed by the wars of its decline, and by the incursions of hordes of barbarians, they found a welcome reception at Byzantium, or Constantinople, whence they subsequently spread into the west of Europe, and were everywhere held in great estimation for their skill in the construction of buildings.

In Italy the associations of architects never entirely ceased, as we may conclude from the many buildings erected there during the domination of the Ostrogoths and the Longobards. Subsequently, when civil order was restored, the Masons of Italy were encouraged and supported by popes, princes, and nobles. And Muratori tells us, in his "*Historia d'Italia,*" that under the Lombard kings the inhabitants of Como were so superior as masons and bricklayers, that the appellation of Magistri Comacini, or Masters from Como, became generic to all those of the profession.

In England, when the Romans took possession of it, the corporations, or colleges of builders, also appeared, who were subsequently continued in the Fraternity of Freemasons, probably established, as Steiglitz thinks, about the middle of the fifth century, after the Romans had left the island. The English Masons were subjected to many adverse difficulties, from the repeated incursions of Scots, Picts, Danes, and Saxons, which impeded their active labors; yet were they enabled to maintain their existence, until, in the year 926, they held that General Assembly at the City of York which framed the constitutions that governed the English Craft for eight hundred years, and which is claimed to be the oldest Masonic record now extant. It is but fair to say, that the recent researches of Bro. Hughan and other English writers have thrown a doubt upon the authenticity of these constitutions, and that the very existence of this York assembly has been denied. But these are historical problems, the true solution of which must be waited for until the further researches of Masonic archæologists shall present us with the necessary data for determining them. Until then it is safer to adhere to the traditional theory, which admits the genuineness of the constitutions and the fact of the assembly.

In France, as in Germany, the Fraternities of Architects originally sprang out of the connection of lay builders with the monks in the era of Charlemagne. The French Masons continued their fraternities throughout the Middle Ages, and erected many cathedrals and public buildings.

We have now arrived at the middle of the eleventh century, tracing the progress of the fraternities of Stonemasons from the time of Charlemagne to that period. At that time all the architecture of Europe was in their hands. Under the distinctive name of *Traveling Freemasons* they passed from nation to nation, constructing churches and cathedrals wherever they were needed. Of their organization and customs Sir Christopher Wren, in his "*Parentalia*," gives the following account:

"Their government was regular, and where they fixed near the building in hand, they made a camp of huts. A surveyor governed in chief; every tenth man was called a warden, and overlooked each nine."

Mr. Hope, who, from his peculiar course of studies, was better acquainted than Mr. Hallam with the history of these Traveling Freemasons, thus speaks, in his "*Essay on Architecture*," of their organization at this time, by which they effected an identity of architectural science throughout all Europe:

"The architects of all the sacred edifices of the Latin Church, wherever such arose—north, south, east, or west—thus derived their science from the same central school; obeyed in their designs the dictates of the same hierarchy; were directed in their constructions by the same principles of propriety and taste; kept up with each other, in the most distant parts to which they might be sent, the most constant correspondence; and rendered every minute improvement the property of the whole body, and a new conquest of the art."

Working in this way, the Stonemasons, as corporations of builders, daily increased in numbers and in power. In the thirteenth century they assumed a new organization. The next chapter will sketch their progress from this new organization at the Cathedral of Strasburg, in the year 1275, until they finally abandoned the operative, and assumed the speculative character, becoming in fact the Free and Accepted Masons of the present day.

———————

BROTHERHOOD.—When our Saviour designated his disciples as his brethren, he implied that there was a close bond of union existing between them, which idea was subsequently carried out by St. Peter, in his direction to "love the brotherhood." Hence the early Christians designated themselves as a *brotherhood*, a relationship unknown to the Gentile religions; and the ecclesiastical and other confraternities of the Middle Ages assumed the same title, to designate an association of men engaged in the same common object, governed by the same rules, and united by an identical interest. The association, or Fraternity of Freemasons, is in this sense called a brotherhood.

TEMPLARISM: ITS DUTY AND ITS SPHERE.

BY ALBERT PIKE.

Seven centuries and a half have passed away since, in 1118, eight French noblemen, uniting themselves into a society, became the Master and Brethren of the Temple. They first displayed the red cross upon the field in 1148; were almost annihilated in storming Ascalon in 1153; their principles were confirmed by the Bull *Omne Datum Optimum*, in 1772; and they fought the great battle of Tiberias in 1187, in which year the Holy City of Jerusalem surrendered to the Infidels. Other crusades were preached, and the soldiery of the Temple fought in the Holy Land until the end of the thirteenth century, by the side, in succession, of Richard Lion-heart of England, and Philip Augustus of France; of Saint Louis and Edward Prince of Wales, at Damietta, Gaza, and Acre; and wherever a blow was to be struck for the Cross against the Crescent.

On the 13th of October, 1307, all the Templars in France were arrested, and on the 11th of March, 1313, the Grand Master was burned. Princes had been members of the Order, and its ambassadors had taken precedence of Christian kings. It had become too powerful by numbers, and wealth, and connections, and it sought to be more powerful still by its influence upon opinions. In the East, the home of Gnosticism, and where the doctrines of Saint John the Apostle were still supreme;—in that Asia Minor of the seven churches, to which Paul, the new apostle, contested the claims of Peter to the pontificate of the Gentile church; in that Orient, of which Patmos, the apocalyptic isle, was a part;—the Templars had learned doctrines not acceptable to the Roman bishops, and it is probable that some of them had accepted those of Manes, and were liable to the pains and penalties denounced against heretics.

To the monarchs of Christendom, all of whom were at that day little more than the deans of the nobility, maintaining a constant struggle against the ambition of their vassals, insecure in their places of power, and without standing armies, the soldiery of the Temple had become a terror by their numbers, their immense possessions, and their unity of organization. For the Order dreamed of an Oriental empire, and sought to obtain, by negotiation, an eastern seaport. It was a standing army of proud, fiery, indomitable warriors, distributed over all Europe, and obedient to the single will of the Grand Master. The thrones and the altars combined against it, and it fell and disappeared in a day. Its pride, ambition, and luxuries, swelled the provocations that caused its ruin. During the centuries that followed, while it was merged in other orders, and wore the mask of Freemasonry, it was, as is usual, chastened and purified by adversity. The advances made by science, the revival of letters, the reopening of the treasures of the ancient Grecian and Oriental wisdom, gave it a deeper and a sounder philosophical doctrine, and a wiser and truer religious creed; and its hereditary desire for vengeance on the despotisms to which its ruin was due, symbolized by the mitre and the crown, led it eagerly to adopt the idea that governments are made for the people, and not the people for governments, upon its first announcement to the world.

If our Order should again become prosperous and powerful, let it avoid the shoals upon which it once suffered shipwreck. Let it become neither haughty, nor vainglorious, nor luxurious, nor useless. The principles which it adopted in adversity, let it adhere to in its better fortunes. Let the enlargement of the Order, and the increase of its members and its Commanderies, be the enlargement of its powers and the confirmation of its desires to benefit mankind, strengthen its hands against all unrighteous usurpation of power by kings, or pontiffs, or popular chiefs, military or civil, and encourage us to hope for the final triumph of liberty, equality, and fraternity, in the sense in which these are understood by the true Freemasonry.

Let us also remember, in striving to benefit our race, that the multitude is in every country instinctive rather than reflective, and can be attached to ideas only by means of forms, and surrenders its prejudices and changes its habits with difficulty. Popular assemblies are not swayed by reason, and legislative majorities are little controlled by any sense of justice. Upon an attempt to combat superstitions, it always seems to the people that religion itself is assailed. Socrates was accused of Atheism before the tribunals; and Jesus was denounced to the authorities as a blasphemer. Wherefore, those that undertake reforms will be wise, if, like Saint Gregory, one of the greatest among the Popes, they do not permit usages to be suppressed. "Purify the temples," he wrote to his missionaries, "but do not destroy them; for so long as the nation shall see its ancient places of prayer standing, it will repair thither by habit, and you will, with the more ease, persuade it to the worship of the true God."

Society has not no right to consider itself enlightened while it regards the abuses of a system as its excellencies, and makes idols of its own prejudices, and looks with horror on attempts to obtain rational reforms as revolutionary projects; nor, while it continues to be ignorant that the criminal instincts are the most frightful of all the mental maladies, and does not comprehend that the disease should be cured, and not put to death, has it any right to consider itself Christian.

Keep these truths always in view in the warfare which you are incessantly to wage against tyrannies. For there are not only tyrannies of thrones and pontificates, but of the people, and parties, and opinion, and of the law. Close around you everywhere you will find evils enough to combat, and it will be well for you if you do not become their ally.

The days have retired but a little way into the past when men were divided into but two classes—the oppresser and oppressed. Then thought was imprisoned; to breathe it was peril, if not death; and it died in the brain where it was born, or was only whispered in the solitude. The obligations of Blue Masonry are retained, that they may incessantly remind us of those wretched days. Now, thought is free as the wind, and the lightning flashes it across the oceans and around the continents. Nations are enfranchised by it, and the golden glories of truth begin to illumine the world. A new power has arisen among men, known as public opinion, with a new weapon—the press. Before it, even the kings recede, and yield to it, and obey its bulls and allocutions, or it shakes down their thrones into the dust.

We should be but cravens, therefore, if we did not persevere. Whatever the evils of to-day in the country in which we live, they are not invincible; for they are neither necessary and inevitable, nor in their nature immortal. Neither are we powerless in the struggle against them, and we are no true knights if we yield to discouragement:

> "The smallest effort is not lost;
> Each wavelet on the ocean tossed
> Aids in the ebb-tide or the flow;
> Each rain-drop helps some flower to blow,
> Each struggle lessens human woe."

HENRY CORNELIUS AGRIPPA—AN UNINITIATED FREE-MASON.

A Biographical Sketch.

BY THE EDITOR.

Henry Cornelius Agrippa, who was distinguished as one of the greatest of occult philosophers, was born in the city of Cologne, on the 14th of September, 1486. He was descended from a noble family, and was personally remarkable for his varied talents and extensive genius. In early youth, he acted as the secretary of the Emperor Maximilian, and subsequently served in the army of the same monarch in Italy, where he received the honor of knighthood for his gallant conduct in the field. He also devoted himself to the study of law and physic, and received from the university the degree of doctorate in each of those faculties. Of his literary attainments, he gives an ample description in one of his epistles, in which he says:

"I am tolerably well skilled in eight languages, and so completely a master of six, that I not only understand and speak them, but can even make an elegant oration, or dictate and translate in them. I have also a pretty extensive knowledge in some abstruse studies, and a general acquaintance with the whole circle of sciences."

There is some vanity in this, but it must be confessed that there was much learning to excuse the weakness. The temper of Agrippa was variable and irascible, and his disposition bold and independent. Hence his pen was continually giving offense, and he was repeatedly engaged in difficulties with his contemporaries, and more especially with the priests, who persecuted him with unrelenting rigor. He traveled much, and visited France, Spain, Italy, and England—sometimes engaged in the delivery of philosophical lectures, sometimes in public employments, and sometimes in the profession of arms.

In 1509 he delivered lectures on Reuchlin's treatise "De Verbo Mirifico," which involved him in a controversy with the Franciscans; and wrote a work on the Excellence of Women, which also gave offense to the ecclesiastics, in consequence of which he was obliged to pass over into England, where he wrote a commentary on St. Paul's Epistles. He afterwards returned to Cologne, where he delivered lectures on divinity. In 1515, we find him reading lectures on Mercurius Trismegistus; but his ill fortune followed him, and he soon left that city, his departure being, according to his biographer, rather like a flight than a retreat.

In 1518 he was at Metz, where he was for some time employed as a syndic and counsellor; but, having refuted a popular notion, that St. Anne had three husbands, and having dared to defend an old woman who had been accused of witchcraft, his old enemies, the monks, once more renewed their ill offices, and he was compelled to leave the city of Metz, bequeathing to it, as his revenge, the character of being the step-mother of all useful learning and virtue.* Thence he retired to Cologne in 1520, and to Geneva in 1521, where poverty seems to have pressed hardly upon him.

In 1524 he was at Lyons, in France, where Francis I. bestowed a pension upon him, and appointed him physician to the king's mother; an office, however, which he lost in 1525, in consequence of twice giving offense to his royal mistress. First, because he expressed his dislike at being employed by her in astrological calculations concerning the

---

* "Omnium bonarum literarum virtutumque noverca."—*Epist. Jun.* 2, 1519.

affairs of France, an employment which he deemed derogatory to a
queen's physician; and next because, when he did make those calculations, he interpreted the stars unfavorably for the king's enterprises.
Agrippa was not of a temper to brook this dismissal with equanimity,
and accordingly we find him, in one of his letters written at this time,
denouncing the queen mother for a most atrocious and perfidious sort of
Jezebel—"*pro atrocissima et perfida quadam Jezabela.*"

In 1528 he repaired to Antwerp, and the year after received from
Margaret of Austria, governess of the low countries, the appointment of
historiographer to the emperor. The History of the Government of
Charles V. was his only contribution to the duties of this office. Soon
after Margaret died, and Agrippa again came into collision with his old
ecclesiastical persecutors, whose resentment was greatly excited by his
treatise " *On the Vanity of the Sciences,*" which he published in 1530,
and another work soon after, written " *On the Occult Philosophy.*" His
pension was discontinued, and in 1531 he was incarcerated in the prison
at Brussels. From this he was, however, soon liberated, and after a few
more adventures, he finally retired to Grenoble, in France, where he
died in 1535; some writers say in abject poverty, and in the public hos-
pital, but this has been denied by Gabriel Naude.

The treatise on occult philosophy is the most important of the works
of Agrippa, and which has given to him the false reputation of being a
hermetic adept and a magician. Thus, Paulus Jovius says that he was
always accompanied by a devil, in the shape of a black dog, wearing a
collar containing some necromantic inscription, and that when he was
about to die he released the dog with an imprecation, after which the
animal fled to the river Soane, into which he leaped and was never heard
of more. Martin del Rio says that when Agrippa traveled, he used to
pay his score at the inns in money which at the time appeared to be
good, but in a few days turned out to be pieces of horn or shell; a tale
which reminds us of one of the stories in the Arabian Nights. The
same author retails another aprocryphal anecdote about a student, who,
during Agrippa's temporary absence, was strangled in the magician's
library by an irate demon, and into whose dead body Agrippa, on his
return, caused the devil to enter, and walk several times across the public
square at Louvain, and finally to drop dead, whereby the death appeared
to be a natural one, and suspicion was thus averted from Agrippa. The
truth is, however, that the treatise on occult philosophy was of so abstruse and mystical a character, that the author found it necessary to write
a key to it, which he reserved for his most intimate friends, and in which
he explained its esoteric meaning.

Masonic historians have very generally attempted to connect Agrippa with that institution, or at least with cognate mystical societies. Thus Gadicke (*Freimaurer-Lexicon*) says:

"A society for the cultivation of the secret sciences, which he founded at Paris, and which extended through Germany, England, France, and Italy, was the first ever established by a learned man, and was the pattern and parent of all subsequent similar societies."

Lenning (*Encyc. der Freimaurerei*) also states that—

"It is reported that Agrippa established in Paris a secret society for the practice of the abstruse sciences, which became the basis of the many mystical associations which have been since originated."

But a writer in the *Monthly Review* (London, vol. XXV, anno 1798, p. 304) is still more explicit on this subject. His language is as follows:

"In the year 1510 Henry Cornelius Agrippa came to London, and, as appears by his correspondence, (*Opuscula t. II, p.* 1073, &c.,) he founded a secret society for alchemical purposes, similar to one which he had previously instituted at Paris, in concert with Landolfo, Brixianus, Xanthus, and other students at that university. The members of these societies did agree on *private signs of recognition;* and they founded, in various parts of Europe, corresponding associations, for the prosecution of the occult sciences. This practice of initiation, or secret incorporation, thus and then first introduced, has been handed down to our own times; and hence apparently the mysterious Eleusinian confederacies now known as the Lodges of Freemasonry."

In 1856 there was published in London a "*Life of Cornelius Agrippa von Nettesheim, Doctor and Knight, commonly known as a Magician. By Henry Morley.*" This is a curious and trustworthy work, and contains a good summary of Agrippa, and interesting notions of the times in which he lived.

As Agrippa has, whether justly or not, been thrown into a connection with Freemasonry, a brief view of his occult philosophy may not be uninteresting. But it must be always borne in mind, that this philosophy was what he called it, "*occulta philosophia*"—occult, hidden; containing, like all the science of the alchemists, more in its inmost recesses than appears on its surface, and that he himself, aware of its esoteric character, had written a key, by which his intimate friends might be able to interpret its concealed meaning and enjoy its fruits. Ragon (*Orthod. Mac., ch. xxviii*) gives a *resume* of the doctrines, from which the following is condensed:

Agrippa said that there were three worlds—the *elementary*, the *celestial*, and the *intellectual*—each subordinate to the one above it. It is possible to pass from the knowledge of one world to that of another, and even to the archetype itself. It is this scale of ascent that constitutes what is called *Magism,* a profound contemplation, embracing nature, quality, substance, virtues, similitudes, differences, the art of uniting, separating, and compounding—in short, the entire operations of the universe. It is a sacred art, which must not be divulged, and to whose reality and certainty the universal connection of all things testifies.

There are abstruse doctrines on the elements, of which each performed a particular function. *Fire,* isolated from all matter, manifests upon it, however, its presence and action; *earth* is the support of the elements and the reservoir of the celestial influences; *water* is the germ of all animals; and *air* is a vital spirit, which penetrates all beings, and gives them consistency and life.

There is a sublime, secret, and necessary cause, which leads to truth.

The world, the heavens, and the stars, have souls, which are in affinity with our own.

The world lives, and has its organs and its senses. This is the microcosm.

Imprecations are of efficacy in attaching themselves to beings, and in modifying them.

Names have a potential quality. Magic has its language, which language is an image of signatures, and hence the effect of invocations, evocations, adjurations, conjurations, and other formulæ.

Numbers are the first cause of the connection of things. To each number is attached a peculiar property—thus: Unity is the beginning and end of all things, but has no beginning nor end itself. God is the monad. The binary is a bad number. The ternary is the soul of the world. The quaternary is the basis of all numbers. The quinary is a powerful number; it is efficacious against poisons and evil spirits. The decade, or denary, is the completion of all things. The intelligence of God is incorruptible, eternal, present everywhere, influencing everything.

The human spirit is corporeal, but its substance is very subtile, and readily unites with the universal spirit, the soul of the world, which is in us.

This is some part of the occult philosophy of Agrippa, who, however, has said, in reference to abstruse theories, almost, if not altogether, unintelligible, like these, that all that the books undertake to teach on the subjects of magic, astrology, and alchemy are false and deceptive, if they are understood in the letter; but that to appreciate them, to draw any good out of them, we must seek the mystic sense in which they are enveloped; a doctrine which applies to Freemasonry, as well as to the hermetic philosophy, and the truth of which is now universally admitted by the learned. The Freemason who expects to find in the abstruse writings of Agrippa anything directly referring to his own institution, will be greatly disappointed; but if he looks in the pages of that profound thinker for lessons of philosophy and ethics, which have a common origin with those that are taught in the Masonic system, his labor will not have been in vain, and he will be disposed to place the wise Cornelius in the same category with Pythagoras, and many other philosophers of the olden time, whom the Craft have delighted to call their ancient brethren, because, without being Freemasons in outward form and ceremony, they have always taught true Masonic doctrine. Hence we think it not inappropriate to give to such unaffiliated teachers the title of " Uninitiated Freemasons," and in this sense we have therefore bestowed it upon Agrippa in the beginning of this sketch.

PROSELYTISM IN MASONRY.

BY THE EDITOR.

Brahmanism is, perhaps, the only religion which is opposed to proselytism. The Brahman seeks no convert to his faith, but is content with that extension of his worship which is derived from the natural increase only of its members. The Jewish Church, perhaps one of the most exclusive, and which has always seemed indifferent to progress, yet provided a special form of baptism for the initiation of its proselytes into the Mosaic rites.

Buddhism, the great religion of the Eastern world, which, notwithstanding the opposition of the leading Brahmans, spread with amazing rapidity over the Oriental nations, so that now it seems the most popular religion of the world, owes its extraordinary growth to the energetic propagandism of Sakya-muni, its founder, and to the same proselyting spirit which he inculcated upon his disciples.

The Christian Church, mindful of the precepts of its divine founder, "Go ye into all the world, and preach the Gospel to every creature," has always considered the work of missions as one of the most important duties of the Church, and owes its rapid increase, in its earlier years, to the proselyting spirit of Paul, and Thomas, and the other apostles.

Mohammedanism, springing up and lingering for a long time in a single family, at length acquired rapid growth among the Oriental nations, through the energetic proselytism of the Prophet and his adherents. But the proselytism of the religion of the New Testament and that of the Koran differed much in character. The Christian made his converts by persuasive accents and eloquent appeals; the Mussulman converted his penitents by the sharp power of the sword. Christianity was a religion of peace, Mohammedanism a religion of war; yet each, though pursuing a different method, was equally energetic in securing converts.

In respect to this doctrine of proselytism, Freemasonry resembles more the exclusive faith of Brahma, than the inviting one of Moses, of Buddha, of Christ, or of Mohammed.

In plain words, Freemasonry is rigorously opposed to all proselytism. While its members do not hesitate, at all proper times and on all fitting occasions, to defend the Institution from all attacks of its enemies, it never seeks, by voluntary laudation of its virtues, to make new accessions of friends, or to add to the number of its disciples.

Nay, it boasts, as a peculiar beauty of its system, that it is a voluntary institution. Not only does it forbid its members to use any efforts to obtain initiates, but actually requires every candidate for admission into its sacred rites to seriously declare, as a preparatory step, that in this voluntary offer of himself he has been unbiased by the improper solicitations of friends. Without this declaration the candidate would be unsuccessful in his application. Although it is required that he should be prompted to solicit the privilege by the favorable opinion which he had conceived of the Institution, yet no provision is made by which that opinion can be inculcated in the minds of the profane; for were a Mason, by any praises of the Order, or any exhibitions of its advantages, to induce any one under such representations to seek admission, he would not only himself commit a grievous fault, but would subject the candidate to serious embarassment at the very entrance of the Lodge.

This Brahmanical spirit of anti-proselytism, in which Masonry differs from every other association, has imprinted upon the Institution certain peculiar features. In the first place, Freemasonry thus becomes, in the most positive form, a voluntary association. Whoever comes within its mystic circle, comes there of his "own free will and accord, and unbiased by the influence of friends." These are the terms on which he is received, and to all the legitimate consequences of this voluntary connection he must submit. Hence comes the axiom, "once a Mason, always a Mason;" that is to say, no man, having once been initiated into its sacred rites, can, at his own pleasure or caprice, divest himself of the obligations and duties which, as a Mason, he has assumed. Coming to us freely and willingly, he can urge no claim for retirement on the plea that he was unduly persuaded, or that the character of the Institution had been falsely represented. To do so, would be to convict himself of fraud and falsehood, in the declarations made by him preliminary to his admission. And if these declarations were indeed false, he at least cannot, under the legal maxim, take advantage of his own wrong. The knot which binds him to the Fraternity has been tied by himself, and is indissoluble. The renouncing Mason may, indeed, withdraw from his connection with a Lodge, but he cannot release himself from his obligations to the regulation, which requires every Mason to be a member of one. He may abstain from all communication with his brethren, and cease to take any interest in the concerns of the Fraternity; but he is not thus absolved from the performance of any of the duties imposed upon him by his original admission into the Brotherhood. A proselyte, persuaded against his will, might claim his right to withdraw; but the voluntary seeker must take and hold what he finds.

Another result of this anti-proselyting spirit of the Institution is, to relieve its members from all undue anxiety to increase its numbers. It is not to be supposed that Masons have not the very natural desire to see the growth of their Order. Towards this end, they are ever ready to defend its character when attacked, to extol its virtues, and to maintain its claims to the confidence and approval of the wise and good. But the growth they wish is not that abnormal one, derived from sudden revivals or ephemeral enthusiasm, where passion too often takes the place of judgment; but that slow and steady, and therefore healthy, growth, which comes from the adhesion of wise and virtuous and thoughtful men, who are willing to join the brotherhood, that they may the better labor for the good of their fellow-men.

Thus it is that we find the addresses of our Grand Masters, the reports of our committees on foreign correspondence, and the speeches of our anniversary orators, annually denouncing the too rapid increase of the Order, as something calculated to affect its stability and usefulness.

And hence, too, the black ball, that antagonist of proselytism, has been long and familiarly called the bulwark of Masonry. Its faithful use is ever being inculcated by the fathers of the Order upon its younger members; and the unanimous ballot is universally admitted to be the most effectual means of preserving the purity of the Institution.

And so, this spirit of anti-proselytism, impressed upon every Mason from his earliest initiation, although not itself a landmark, has come to be invested with all the sacredness of such a law, and Freemasonry stands out alone, distinct from every other human association, and proudly proclaims, "Our portals are open to all the good and true, but we ask no man to enter."

BEAUTY.—Winkelman has a fine idea, when he says that "perfect beauty, like the purest water, must have no peculiarity."

CONSCIENCE.—A Welch proverb says, that conscience is only the eye of God in the soul of man.

IS IGNORANCE A CRIME IN MASONRY?

BY JOHN EDWIN MASON, M. D.

All Masons naturally seek for "more light." If they love the principles of Freemasonry, they cherish a desire to learn more of the history and literature of such a noble Order, and become acquainted with the law, usages, and jurisprudence governing Freemasonry at the present day.

They desire to give information to their less informed brethren, who have just been obligated on its holy altars.

As "education makes the man," so it also makes the Mason. The obligation taken on the holy altar does not virtually make a man a Mason. The Masonic world acknowledges him as such, but if he has no knowledge of Masonry, and does not seek to obtain any, he is simply a fraud upon the Craft, and has no rights that Masons are bound to respect. He is a living monument of the folly, so common at the present day, of making Masons of all applicants, without regarding their mental qualifications. A wide distinction should be made between candidates for Masonry and the idiotic asylum.

Mr. Pointless makes application to be made a Mason, because he finds that Masonry is very popular, and he thinks he will be able to sell more cabbages in the market. A correct prognosis would make very little difference between his head and the cabbage heads he sells in the market. Both are harmless specimens of verdancy, unequalled in the vegetable kingdom.

Mr. Pointless never had an idea above an oyster in all his life. Two distinct ideas never crept into that head at the same time, because it would cause an explosion. The boiler would burst, like any other boiler. It was a wise provision of nature that such boilers should burst.

He fully realizes that—

> "The wise are happy, nature to explore;
> The fool is happy that he knows no more."

The committee call upon Mr. Pointless, and find him an honest, truthful, upright man, with no bad habits, and an exemplary member of Rev. Mr. Blowhard's church. The committee make a favorable report, and Mr. Pointless is made a Mason in due and ancient form.

No one could measure his appreciation of the degrees by the quart or gallon. As years roll by, his knowledge of Masonry is just about the same as that he possesses of the differential calculus, of Socrates, or Hippocrates. He cannot be stimulated to learn anything, because he invariably says he "has no larnin'." He dies in good standing, without ever having been able to prove himself a Mason, or even give the passwords.

The question arises, when Mr. Pointless dies, did Masonry make him a better man, or make him serve his fellow-men as the Bible teaches? All must reply in the negative. Mr. Pointless did not profit by the valuable lessons taught in Masonry, because he knew nothing about them, and was too ignorant to learn them. But can he be blamed for his ignorance? Most assuredly; for in this country schools are free, and education flows like the mountain streamlet, and he who refuses to drink at its fountain is a criminal.

The ignorance of such a man casts a stain upon Masonry. No such person can be considered a worthy candidate. His life was not only a blank to Masonry, but an actual disgrace. The dangerous classes are always ignorant men. Mobs and riots originate among these classes. Ignorant men are dangerous to Masonry. They must be kept out. In the dark days of anti-masonry, it was the ignorant men in the Craft who rose up and took the life of our beloved Order. If dark days come again, the same class will do the same thing. We can only judge the future by the past. Anti-masonic conventions have been held the past year in Pittsburg, Pennsylvania; Syracuse, New York; Worcester, Massachusetts; and in various other places. The cloud is now no larger than a man's hand, but it may increase, until it bursts into a storm that will sweep all before it, as it did forty years ago. To be fore-warned is to be forearmed.

There are too many drones in the Masonic hive, whose negligence is only surpassed by their ignorance. They have passed through all the degrees, but never visit their Lodges, Chapters, Councils, or Command-eries. They howl once a year, when they pay their dues to the secretary, otherwise they do not disturb the harmony of the Craft. As they joined Masonry in order to benefit themselves, they never give a dollar for char-ity. They look upon Masonry as a popular Order, but should a storm arise and its popularity be shaken, these men would be the first to leave the ship. Then they would declare that they never had a good opinion of it. Such hypocrites are always ignorant men, and their ignorance is a crime in Masonry.

We have also a class of sincere and enthusiastic Masons, who are not ignorant in one sense, yet they are in another. They have committed to memory the ritual, so they can confer almost any degree, and yet they know so little of the history, literature, and jurisprudence of Masonry, that any profane would make them blush for shame if he asked them very common questions. Their senseless gabble over the ritual makes the Craft call them "Parrot Masons," because they learn Masonry as the parrot learns a language. Darwin would say that their origin could be traced back to a parrot. With contracted and narrow ideas about Masonry, they oppose the publication of anything on Masonry in newspapers or periodicals, and have a cold chill whenever they see a word in print about Masonry. They have an idea that Masonry is something like a black coal-hole, in which no light should enter. They foster ignorance, by opposing everybody in the Order whose ideas are not as narrow as their own. They oppose Masonic books and papers, because they educate Masons to know more than they ever hope to possess. All their long lives they have been

> "Dropping buckets into empty wells,
> And growing old in drawing nothing up."

Some of the most ignorant even go so far as to oppose the calling of Masonic meetings through the daily newspapers, or the simple announcements what degrees would be worked. They can give no reason for such foolish and ridiculous assurances, and only refer to the fact, that King Solomon did not publish such notices, as no newspapers then existed! If they followed King Solomon in other things as closely as in this, they would each possess more wives than Brigham Young. Would that be Masonic also?

> "Where ignorance is bliss
> 'T is folly to be wise."

All the above-named classes need "more light," in accordance with the strict meaning of that term in Masonry. This light is simply more knowledge. The great question to meet now, face to face, is how this Masonic information can be imparted. It is, perhaps, the most important question now discussed by learned Masons all over the world.

A diagnosis of this disease in Masonry has been made, the prognosis given, and now the remedy must be applied. There is a specific that stands ready to cure ignorance in any form, no matter how virulent. It is reading, study, and *thinking*. If Masons will only do their own thinking, and not hire it, done by the job, there will be a radical change. If they will study Masonry as a science, they will glean rich gems from her precious mines. If they will read the history and literature of Masonry, they will be astonished to find so rich a harvest. Well-informed Masons often say that Masonry has no literature. The proceedings of Grand Lodges, Chapters, Councils, and Commanderies all over the world, the different Masonic events that are celebrated by addresses, orations, poems, &c., all furnish a rich current literature of Freemasonry.

The reports on foreign correspondence, in all the Grand Bodies in the United States, compare favorably with our best magazine literature. Here is a rich field, in which to gather information, and to obtain all the Masonic news in every State. And yet how few Masons carefully peruse them! The writer reads annually over three thousand pages of proceedings of Grand Bodies, and two thousand pages of Masonic addresses, poems, and newly-published books on Masonry, and yet feels ashamed that he only has time to read these five thousand pages.

The other sources of Masonic information are all good, but cannot compare with a monthly magazine. This is unquestionably the best. Such varied information is obtained, that any Mason who takes a monthly or weekly Masonic publication, and reads it carefully, is generally the best educated on all Masonic subjects, and knows also what is being done by his fraters abroad. He finds answers to all the questions that naturally occur to an inquiring mind, and finds it his best Masonic companion.

Such a magazine as "MACKEY'S NATIONAL FREEMASON" will do more to educate the ignorant than the Craft can at first realize. It will dispense light to the needy, and refresh every thirsty Mason who is seeking truth. It is a fountain of knowledge, where all can slake their thirst. As it breaks the dark clouds of ignorance, it also dries up the corrupting influences that make crime in Masonry. Ignorance and crime are synonymous terms. It lays them both in one grave, side by side. *Requiescant in pace.*

There are three thousand Masons in the city of Washington, who ought to hail the appearance of this new light in Masonry as the traveler hails the first purple tints of dawn that gild the eastern horizon. As it unfolds monthly such a storehouse of knowledge, they will all finally exclaim, that "ignorance *is* a crime in Masonry."

BACULUS: THE STAFF OF THE GRAND MASTER OF THE TEMPLARS.

BY ALBERT G. MACKEY, M. D.

In ecclesiology, *baculus* is the name given to the pastoral staff carried by a bishop or an abbot as the insignia of his dignity and authority. In pure Latinity, *baculus* means a long stick or staff, which was commonly carried by travelers, by shepherds, or by infirm and aged persons, and afterwards, from affectation, by the Greek philosophers. In early times, this staff, made a little longer, was carried by kings and persons in authority, as a mark of distinction, and was thus the origin of the royal sceptre. The Christian Church, borrowing many of its usages from antiquity, and alluding also, it is said, to the sacerdotal power, which Christ conferred when he sent the apostles to preach, commanding them to take with them staves, adopted the pastoral staff, to be borne by a bishop, as symbolical of his power to inflict pastoral correction; and Durandus says, "By the pastoral staff is likewise understood the authority of doctrine. For by it the infirm are supported, the wavering are confirmed, those going astray are drawn to repentance." Catalin also says, "That the baculus, or episcopal staff, is an ensign not only of honor, but also of dignity, power, and pastoral jurisdiction."

The transmission of episcopal ensigns from bishops to the heads of ecclesiastical associations was not difficult in the Middle Ages; and hence it afterwards became one of the insignia of abbots and the heads of confraternities connected with the Church, as a token of the possession of powers of ecclesiastical jurisdiction.

Now, as the Papal Bull *Omne actum Optimum*, invested the Grand Master of the Templars with almost episcopal jurisdiction over the Priests of his Order, he bore the *baculus*, or pastoral staff, as a mark of that jurisdiction, and thus it became a part of the Grand Master's insignia of office; or, as St. Bernard has it, in the *Regula* of the Order, attributed to his pen, "The Master *ought to hold the staff and the rod in his hand;* that is to say, the staff, that he may support the infirmities of the weak; and the rod, that he may, with the zeal of rectitude, strike down the vices of delinquents."

The *baculus* of the bishop, the abbot, and the confraternities was not precisely the same in form. The earliest episcopal staff terminated in a globular knob, or a tau cross. This was, however, soon replaced by the simple curved termination, which resembles and is called a crook, in allusion to that used by shepherds to draw back and recall the sheep of their flock which have gone astray, thus symbolizing the expression of Christ, "I am the good Shepherd, and know my sheep, and am known of mine."

The *baculus* of the abbot does not differ in form from that of a bishop, but as the bishop carries the curved part of his staff pointing forward, to show the extent of his episcopal jurisdiction, so the abbot carries his pointing backward, to signify that his authority is limited to his monastery.

The *baculi*, or staves of the confraternities, were surmounted by small tabernacles, with images or emblems, on a sort of carved cap, having reference to the particular guild or confraternity by whom they were borne.

The *baculus* of the Knights Templars, which was borne by the Grand Master as the ensign of his office, in allusion to his *quasi* episcopal jurisdiction, is described and delineated in Muenter, Burnes, Addison, and all the other authorities, as a staff, on the top of which is an octagonal figure, surmounted with a cross patee. The cross, of course, refers to the Christian character of the Order, and the octagon alludes, it is said, to the eight beatitudes of our Saviour in his Sermon on the Mount.

The pastoral staff is variously designated, by ecclesiastical writers, as *virga, ferula, cambutta, crocia,* and *pedum.* From *crocia,* whose root is the Latin *crux,* and the Italian *croce,* a cross, we get the English *crozier.*

Pedum, another name of the *baculus,* signifies, in pure Latinity, a shepherd's crook, and thus strictly carries out the symbolic idea of a pastoral charge. Hence, looking to the pastoral jurisdiction of the Grand Master of the Templars, his staff of office is described under the title of "*pedum magistrale seu patriarchale;*" that is, a "magisterial or patriarchal staff," in the *Statuta Commilitonum Ordinis Templi,*" or the "Statutes of the Fellow-soldiers of the Order of the Temple, as a part of the investiture of the Grand Master, in the following words:

"*Pedum magistrale seu patriarchale, aureum, in cacumine cujus crux Ordinis super orbem exaltatur;*" that is, "a magisterial or patriarchal staff of gold, on the top of which is a cross of the Order, surmounting an orb or globe." (*Stat.* xxviii, art. 358.) But of all these names, *baculus* is the one more commonly used by writers to designate the Templar pastoral staff.

In the year 1859, if we are correct in our recollection, this staff of office was first adopted at Chicago, by the Templars of the United States, during the Grand Mastership of the late lamented Sir William B. Hubbard. But, unfortunately, at that time it received the name of *abacus,* a misnomer, which has continued to the present day, and which has unhappily gained some strength from its adoption by Bro. Robert Macoy in his "Cyclopædia of Freemasonry," who defines the *abacus* as being, "in the Templar system of Masonic Knighthood, the name of the Grand Master's staff of office," and he quotes as his authority a literary blunder of Sir Walter Scott, so that it has fallen to the lot of American Masons to perpetuate, in the use of this word, an error of the great novelist, resulting from his too careless writing, at which he would himself have been the first to smile, had his attention been called to it.

Abacus, in mathematics, denotes an instrument or table used for calculation, and in architecture an ornamental part of a column; but it nowhere, in English or Latin, or any known language, signifies any kind of a staff.

Sir Walter Scott, who, undoubtedly was thinking of *baculus,* in the hurry of the moment and a not improbable confusion of words and thoughts, wrote *abacus,* when, in his novel of Ivanhoe, he describes the Grand Master, Lucas Beaumanoir, as bearing in his hand "that singular *abacus,* or staff of office," committed a very gross, but not very uncommon, literary blunder, of a kind that is quite familiar to those who are conversant with the results of rapid composition.

A contemporary writer of some celebrity, Mr. Robert Grant White, has recently found it necessary to explain, in the *Galaxy*, a similar blunder committed by himself. In treating of the authors of the *Federalist*, he had placed among them the name of Monroe, instead of Madison, an error which clearly cannot be attributed to ignorance, and on which he makes the following apposite remarks:

"And yet I, knowing, of course, perfectly well, as I had known for years, who were the authors of the "*Federalist*," wrote *Monroe* instead of *Madison*, and read it in proof, and the proof-reader at Riverside read *Monroe*, and never raised a query as to a point on which any grammar-school boy is informed, and as to which he, like me, had had recent and reiterated reminders. By a perverse action of the mind, which is much more common than it is supposed to be, I had written *Monroe* when I thought *Madison*, and both the proof-reader and I, in reading proof, saw what was in our mind's eye, and not that which was before our bodies. This kind of error is one of the commonest. It prevails as to matters of fact, but not as to those of thought. People continually use the wrong name or the wrong word in speech, and even in writing, when they know well the right one." (*Galaxy*, vol. II, No. 6, p. 789.)

This was precisely the case with Sir Walter Scott. We say nothing of his proverbial carelessness; he is not often quoted as authority in terms of heraldry, nor often cited in defence of the accuracy of an expression. White's explanation is sufficient for us. As he wrote *Monroe* when he thought *Madison*, so the author of Ivanhoe wrote *abacus* when he thought *baculus*. And an historical society would have as much right to quote Mr. White as authority, that Monroe wrote some of the numbers of the *Federalist*, as a body of Templars has to quote Sir Walter Scott as their authority for calling the Grand Master's staff an *abacus*. The one would not be a whit more absurd than the other. Each would be a blunder, based upon a blunder.

Will not Bro. Macoy, after this explanation, strike out his incorrect definition from the next edition of his Cyclopædia; and will not American Templars, hereafter, cease to confound a mathematical table for calculation and the crowning member of an architectural column, with their Grand Master's staff of office, now so ably wielded by one of the most accomplished Masons of our country?

THE SOUL'S STRUGGLES.—The soul shall never gain a victory without a conflict; never enjoy a triumph without a struggle; never wear a wreath that she has not won.—*Rev. Chas. T. Brooks.*

THE MASON'S HOLY HOUSE.

BY ALBERT PIKE.

We have a Holy House to build,
  A Temple splendid and divine,
To be with glorious memories filled;
  Of Right and Truth to be the shrine.
How shall we build it strong and fair,—
This Holy House of Praise and Prayer,
  Firm-set and solid, grandly great?
How shall we all its rooms prepare
  For use, for ornament, for state?

Our God hath given the wood and stone,
  And we must fashion them aright,
Like those who toiled on Lebanon,
  Making the labor their delight:
This House, this Palace, this God's Home,
This Temple with its lofty dome,
  Must be in all proportions fit,
That heavenly messengers may come
  To lodge with those who tenant it.

Build squarely up the stately walls,
  The two symbolic columns raise,
And let the lofty courts and halls
  With all their golden glories blaze.
There, in the Kadosh-Kadoshim,
Between the broad-winged cherubim,
  Where the Shekinah once abode,
The heart shall raise its daily hymn
  Of gratitude and love to God.

DUTY.—No creature should breathe the breath of life without adding his mite to the amount of duties performed, which existence claims as its due. However little, each may do something towards working the great machine, if it be but to lift a straw or a pebble from the path of the great men who best can put the springs in motion. Very few of us can be great, but all may be useful.—*Frazer's Magazine.*

ACCORDING to an estimate, the destruction of property in Paris, including houses, furniture, &c., is valued at thirty-two million pounds. Merchandise to the amount of twenty-four million pounds is also said to have been destroyed.

OLD RECORDS OF FREEMASONRY.

BY THE EDITOR.

In the prospectus of the NATIONAL FREEMASON, we announced that the publication of rare and valuable Masonic documents would constitute a part of the plan. In making this announcement, we were well aware that no part of the magazine would be more valuable, or more interesting, in a literary and historical point of view, than this proposed collection of the old records of Freemasonry.

The early history of Masonry, as written by Anderson, Preston, Smith, Calcott, and writers of that generation, was little more than a collection of fables, so absurd as to excite the smile of every reader, or bare statements of incidents, without any authority to substantiate their genuineness.

The recent writers on the same subject have treated it in a very different manner, and one that gives to the investigation of the early annals of Freemasonry a respectable position in the circle of historic studies. Much of the increased value that is given in the present day to Masonic history is derivable from the fact that, ceasing to repeat the gratuitous statements of the older writers, some of whom have not hesitated to make Adam a Grand Master, and Eden the site of a Lodge, our students of this day are drawing their conclusions from, and establishing their theories on, the old records, which Masonic archæology is, in this generation, bringing to light. Hence, one of these students (Bro. Woodford, of England,) has said, that when we begin to investigate the real facts of Masonic history, "not only have we to discard at once much that we have held tenaciously and taught habitually, simply resting on the reiterated assertions of others, but we shall also find, that we have to get rid of what, I fear, we must call 'accumulated rubbish,' before we can see clearly how the great edifice of Masonic history, raised at last on sure and good foundations, stands out clearer to the sight, and even more honorable to the builders, from those needful, if preparatory labors."

Anderson tells us that in the year 1719, at some of the private Lodges, "several very valuable manuscripts concerning the Fraternity, their Lodges, Regulations, Charges, Secrets, and Usages, were too hastily burnt by some scrupulous brothers, that those papers might not fall into strange hands."

In the last quarter of a century the archæologists of Masonry have labored very diligently and successfully to disinter from the old Lodges, libraries, and museums, many of these ancient manuscripts, and much light has thus been thrown upon the early history of Freemasonry.

1. One of the earliest of these old manuscripts is one entitled " *Constituciones artis gemetrie secundum Euclydum,*" which is really the old Con-

stitutions of Masonry written in a poetical form. Its date is not later than the middle of the fifteenth century, and from the copy on vellum, (the only one extant,) in the British Museum, Mr. Halliwell published an edition in 1840. This document is exceedingly valuable, as containing the first copy of the Masonic laws, and also as showing, incidentally, the close connection between the English and German Masons of the Middle Ages. Dr. Oliver thinks that this is the Constitution of York, adopted in 926, but the truth of this theory is denied by some later writers.

2. Then we have the *Constitutions of the Strasburg Masons* in 1459, which have been published by Kloss and Findel.

3. The oldest English Masonic MS., after Halliwell's, is that commonly called *Matthew Cooke's*, because an almost *fac simile* copy of it was edited by that gentleman in 1862. This manuscript, which is also in the British Museum, is supposed to have been written in the year 1490.

4. The *Lansdowne MS.*, printed in the *London Freemasons' Magazine* for February, 1858. Its title is, "*The True Order of Masonrie*," and the date is about 1560.

5. The *Schaw MS.*, which contains the "Statutes and Ordinances to be observed by all the Masters Masons" in Scotland. Its date is 1598. The MS. is contained in the Lodge of Edinburgh, and was first published by Laurie, in his "*History of Freemasonry*." This is a valuable document, showing the identity, at that time, of the English and Scotch Masons, as the Halliwell MS. does that of the German and English.

6. The *St. Clair MSS.*, in possession of the Grand Lodge of Scotland, and also published by Laurie. They relate, like the *Schaw MS.*, to Scottish Masonry, and have a date of about 1600 and 1628.

7. The *Eglinton MS.*, so called from its having been discovered some years ago in the charter-chest of Eglinton Castle. Its date is 1599, and it also refers to the Masonry of Scotland. It has been recently printed, for the first time, by Bro. Hughan, in his "*Unpublished Records of the Craft*."

8. The *Sloane MS.*, in the British Museum. Its date is 1646, and it contains the history and the constitutions of Masonry. We are indebted again to Bro. Hughan for the publication of this valuable document.

9. The *Harleian MS.* This is preserved in the British Museum, and its date is 1650. It is entitled "*The Free Masons' Orders and Constitutions*." It has been published, for the first time, by Bro. Hughan.

10. *The Edinburgh Kilwinning MS.* Its date is about 1670. It is the property of the Mother Kilwinning Lodge of Scotland, and was made known to the Craft by Brother D. Murray Lyon, from whose copy it was published by Brother Hughan.

11. *The Alnwick MS.*, whose date is 1701, under the title of " *The Masons' Constitution.*" It gives the legendary history and the charges of the Order.

12. *The Dowland MS.*, whose date is believed to be 1550. It derives its name from Mr. James Dowland, who transcribed it for the " *Gentlemen's Magazine,*" in which work it was published in the year 1815.

13. *The Preston MS.*, first published by Preston, in his " *Illustrations of Masonry,*" and having a date not later than 1686. This MS. contains the charges at the installation of the Master of the Lodge, and the charges at making Masons.

14. *The Locke MS.* was printed in " *The Gentlemen's Magazine,*" in 1753, and is said to have been written in the reign of Henry VI. The best Masonic writers doubt the authenticity of this document.

15. *The Charter of Cologne.* This MS. is dated 1535, and was first published in 1819, by Prince Frederick of Nassau, who was then Grand Master of the National Grand Lodge of Holland. This document, if authentic, would be very valuable and interesting; but Masonic authorities are divided on the question of its genuineness. The more general inclination is to believe it a forgery.

There are many other old records, some of which have never yet been published, and the collection forms a mass of material absolutely necessary for the proper investigation of Masonic history. Every Mason who desires to know the true condition of the Fraternity during the last three or four centuries, and who would learn the connection between the Stonemasons of the Middle Ages and the Free and Accepted Masons of the present day, so as perfectly to understand the process by which the Institution became changed from an operative art to a speculative science, should attentively read and thoroughly digest these ancient records of the Brotherhood.

To assist in the accomplishment of this object, it is our intention to publish, from time to time, in the pages of this magazine, the most important of these Masonic records, accompanied with explanatory notes, so as to make them both instructive and interesting to our readers. We shall commence this task by the publication in the next number of the *Matthew Cooke MS.*

At a banquet, when solving enigmas was one of the diversions, Alexander the Great said to his courtiers, "What is that which did not come last year, has not come this year, and will not come next year?" A distressed officer, starting up, said, "It certainly must be our arrears of pay." The king was so diverted, that he commanded him to be paid, and also increased his salary.

THE ROYAL ARCH BANNERS.

BY ALBERT G. MACKEY, M. D.

Much difficulty has been experienced by ritualists in reference to the true colors and proper arrangements of the banners used in an American Chapter of Royal Arch Masons. It is admitted that they are four in number, and that their colors are blue, purple, scarlet, and white; and it is known, too, that the devices on these banners are a lion, an ox, a man, and an eagle; but the doubt is constantly arising as to the relation between these devices and these colors, and as to which of the former is to be appropriated to each of the latter. The question, it is true, is one of mere ritualism, but it is important that the ritual should be always uniform, and hence the object of the present article is to attempt the solution of this question.

The banners used in a Royal Arch Chapter are derived from those which are supposed to have been borne by the twelve tribes of Israel during their encampment in the wilderness, to which reference is made in the second chapter of the Book of Numbers, and the second verse: "Every man of the children of Israel shall pitch by his own standard." But as to what were the devices on the banners, or what were their various colors, the Bible is absolutely silent. To the inventive genius of the Talmudists are we indebted for all that we know or profess to know on this subject. These mystical philosophers have given to us with wonderful precision the various devices which they have borrowed from the death-bed prophesy of Jacob, and have sought, probably in their own fertile imaginations, for the appropriate colors. ·

The English Royal Arch Masons, whose system differs very much from that of their American Companions, display in their Chapters the twelve banners of the tribes in accordance with the Talmudic devices and colors. These have been very elaborately described by Dr. Oliver, in his "*Historical Landmarks*," and beautifully exemplified by Companion Harris, in his "*Royal Arch Tracing Boards*."

But our American Royal Arch Masons, as we have seen, use only four banners, being those attributed by the Talmudists to the four principal tribes—Judah, Ephraim, Reuben, and Dan. The devices on these banners are respectively a lion, an ox, a man, and an eagle. As to this there is no question; all authorities, such as they are, agreeing on this point. But, as has been before said, there is some diversity of opinion as to the colors of each, and necessarily as to the officers by whom they should be borne.

Some of the Targumists, or Jewish biblical commentators, say that the color of the banner of each tribe was analogous to that of the stone which represented that tribe in the breast-plate of the high priest. If this were correct, then the colors of the banners of the four leading tribes would be red and green—namely: red for Judah, Ephraim, and Reuben; and green for Dan; these being the colors of the precious stones sardonyx, ligure, carbuncle, and chrysolite, by which these tribes were represented in the high priest's breast-plate. Such an arrangement would not, of course, at all suit the symbolism of the American Royal Arch banners.

Equally unsatisfactory is the disposition of the colors derived from the arms of speculative Masonry, as first displayed by Dermot, in his "*Ahiman Rezon*," which is familiar to all American Masons, from the copy published by Cross, in his "*Hieroglyphic Chart*." In this piece of blazonry, the two fields occupied by Judah and Dan are *azure*, or blue, and those of Ephriam and Reuben are *or*, or golden yellow; an appropriation of colors altogether uncongenial with Royal Arch symbolism.

We must, then, depend on the Talmudic writers solely, for the disposition and arrangement of the colors and devices of these banners. From their works, we learn that the color of the banner of Judah was white; that of Ephraim scarlet; that of Reuben purple; and that of Dan blue; and that the devices of the same tribes were respectively the lion, the ox, the man, and the eagle.

Hence, under this arrangement—and it is the only one upon which we can depend—the four banners in a Chapter of Royal Arch Masons, working in the American Rite, must be distributed as follows among the banner-bearing officers:

1st. An eagle, on a blue banner. This represents the tribe of Dan, and is borne by the Grand Master of the first vail.

3d. A man, on a purple banner. This represents the tribe of Reuben, and is borne by the Grand Master of the second vail.

2d. An ox, on a scarlet banner. This represents the tribe of Ephraim, and is borne by the Grand Master of the third vail.

4th. A lion, on a white banner. This represents the tribe of Judah, and is borne by the Royal Arch Captain.

SOLDIERS OF CHRIST.—*Milites Christi*, is the title by which St. Bernard addressed his exhortations to the Knights Templars. They are also called in some of the old documents "*Militia Templi Salomonis*"—The Army of the Temple of Solomon; but their ancient statutes were entitled "*Regula pauperum commilitonum Templi Salomonis*"—The Rule of the poor fellow-soldiers of the Temple of Solomon; and this is the title by which they are now most generally designated.

𝔗𝔥𝔢 𝔉𝔞𝔪𝔦𝔩𝔶 ℭ𝔦𝔯𝔠𝔩𝔢.

"THE STRANGEST ADVENTURE."

"Yes, I could tell you plenty of stories like that; I've seen a few adventures in my time."

"You have, indeed; but won't you give me a few more? It's early yet."

We were sitting in the half-demolished summer-house of a little village inn, on the coast of Brittany—in all probability the only wakeful inhabitants of the whole place, for sitting up till eleven p. m. is an enormity unknown in that primitive region. My companion's stern swarthy face and tangled black beard, seen beneath the uncertain light of the rising moon, might have made him appear, to any person of unsteady nerves, rather an "uncanny" comrade for a midnight *tête-a-tête;* but in spite of his repellant manner and miner-like roughness of speech, there was an indescribable *something* in his tone and bearing, which convinced me that, however he might have fallen, or been forced into his present nondescript way of life, he had (to use the common phrase) "been a gentleman once." This, however, was mere conjecture on my part; for in all the marvellous diorama of personal adventure which he had spread before me— riotous revels in Australian taverns, succeeded by days of deadly peril in Antarctic seas; fights with pirates in the Straits of Malacca, following upon weeks of luxurious indolence amid the lotus-eaters of Brazil; sledge-drives across Russian steppes, and bear-hunts in American forests—there was not the slightest hint at his early life or original station in society. It was at the close of a vivid description of a hurricane off Cape Horn that my Ulysses paused in his narrative, and I now reiterated my request for another page from this eventful autobiography.

"What! not tired yet? It's not every one that could stand hearing a fellow talk so long about himself."

"Well," said I, "I'll only ask you for one more; tell me the strangest adventure you ever had."

The wanderer started slightly, and then said, in an altered voice, "You've made a better bargain than you think for; I *will* tell you the strangest of all, and let us see how you like it. I don't ask you to believe it, because I know that when you put these sort of things into books people laugh, and talk of Baron Munchausen, and all that. ·I've read the Baron," he went on, noticing my look of surprise, "and many another

from the camp, till at last (about noon it must have been, by the sun) I
began to feel hungry, and commenced looking very hard at my 'damper'
and cold mutton, which lay upon a log t'other side of the tent. 'Well,'
thought I, 'it's a queer thing for a man to be starved this way, with food
before his eyes!' But the moment I thought it, something cold seemed
to clutch my heart and squeeze it all together. I tried to put it away by
saying to myself, 'This'll go off soon, of course it will;' but at that minute it flashed across me, as if some one had written it in letters of fire all
over the place, 'And supposing it *doesn't* go off; WHAT THEN?'

"It was then I began to feel frightened for the first time. I turned
sick all at once, as if I were going to die, and likely enough I may have
fainted, for the next thing I remember, there was a great silence all over
the camp; and by that I knew that the men were having their dinner,
and that it must be late in the afternoon. As night came on, I began to
feel very bad every way. So long as the sun was shining, and the sound
of the picking and shoveling went on, the light, and the noise, and the
feeling of having lots of people close to me, kept me up a bit; but when
the sounds died away little by little, and the darkness came all round, as
if it were locking me in, I felt as cast down and helpless as a child lost
in a great town. However, my hunger made me savage-like, and that
held me up; for so long as there's strength enough for anger in a man,
he's got a chance; it's when he *can't* feel savage that his heart's broken.
Only I kept always wishing that something would break the silence; and
at last something *did* with a vengeance, for a lot of the horrible dingoes
commenced howling. And so they kept on, and worked me up till I
felt as if I'd give anything to have just one blow at them, no matter what
came after; for what with the hunger, and the lying still so long, and the
howling of these brutes, I'd got so mad, that I'd have liked to kill *something*, no matter what it was. And so the night wore away—a dreary
night for me?"

While he was speaking the moon had become gradually obscured, and
we were wrapped in a shadowy dimness that harmonized well with the
gloomy recital, to which the deepening somberness of his tone lent additional horror.

"The sun rose at last, but it brought no bright morning hope with it;
only the same weary helplessness, which seemed as if it had lasted for
days and days—for I had lost all count of time. When the noise of the
diggings began again, I almost wished it would leave off, much as I had
wished for it before; for it sent a kind of horror through me to think
of the hundreds of men so near, any one of whom would have run like
lightning to help me, if he'd only known of the scrape I was in—while
I lay dumb and dying close by. Ay, *dying!* It was no use shamming

hopeful any longer; for now I began to feel a gnawing and tugging in my inside, as if the teeth of a wolf were tearing it; and I knew what that meant, for I'd felt it before, only not so bad. I wouldn't have minded so much, if I could only have screamed, or flung myself about, or *anything* to show what I felt; but to lie there, stock-still and speechless, it was horrible."

A shudder, which I could see in the uncertain light, shook his strong frame as he proceeded.

"As the sun grew hotter, the flies began to swarm; and, as I watched them, it struck me all of a sudden, what a way I should be in, supposing they attacked me; for, as I was then, they might have sucked every drop of my blood before I could have stirred a finger. I knew something of what Australian bush-flies could do, for I'd once stumbled on the body of a shepherd who had been tied to a tree by the bush-rangers, and left. However, luckily for me, there was something else in the tent that tempted them more, and that was the food I'd left lying on the log. In a second they were down on it; all the meat turned black at once, as if with a shower of soot, and their buzzing was like the wind blowing through a row of wires. You'd laugh at me, stranger, if I were to tell you how savage that sight made me; for, of course, you'll say I ought to have been mighty glad to get off so cheap; but, oh! to see those accursed vermin gorging themselves before my eyes, while I, a *man*, lay starving! I tell you, all that I felt before was nothing to it!

"Towards afternoon there began a kind of whispering and humming in my ears, getting louder bit by bit. It wasn't the flies, for they were all gone; it was what comes to one on the second or third day of starving to death, and I knew it. Some of my mates that were starved up country used to keep putting their hands to their ears for awhile before they died, saying they heard something whispering to them. It got stronger and stronger, till the sound seemed to shape itself into an old song that a man I was with in Brazil kept crooning over just before *he* died. The song was all about a party going across the desert to look for some men that were lost; but the verse that rang in my head then was this:

> "'And never a man, and never a beast,
> They met on their desolate way;
> But the bleaching bones in the hungry sand
> Said all that a tongue could say.'

And so it kept going over and over, till at last I fairly went off, half slept and half fainted.

"It was late when I awoke, and I can't tell you how I felt at seeing the sun setting again. As the light faded, I felt as if my life was going

out along with it, and when it dipped below the horizon, I was ready to
start up and stretch out my arms to hold it back, if I'd had the strength.
And such a night as that second night was, good Heaven! There's a
verse somewhere in the Bible that speaks of 'a horror of great darkness;'
I learned it at school, but I never knew what it really meant till then.
This time there was no howling of dingoes, no noise of any sort; all was
deadly still, as if the world itself, with all that lived and breathed in it,
were dead, and I alone kept living, living on. I suppose I must have
been getting light-headed with hunger and weakness, for I began to fancy
all sorts of queer things. First, I thought I was nailed down in a coffin,
and that if I could only move or scream, or even speak, the lid would fly
open; but I couldn't. Then it seemed as if I were at the bottom of the
sea, and the weight of water above pressed me down, till I could hardly
breathe. All at once I was startled out of my fancies by a sound close
to the tent, the like of which I never heard before or since: a low moan-
ing cry, that sounded like 'All alone! all alone!' over and over again. I
can't tell to this day whether I really heard it, or only fancied it; but at
the time it gave me such a horror, that I nearly went mad.

"The third morning came, and found me nearly at my last. The
gnawing pain was gone, and instead of it had come a pleasant drowsiness,
like what a man feels when he falls down to sleep in the snow. All the
morning I lay in a kind of dream, thinking of nothing, fearing nothing;
as quiet as a child at its mother's breast; till all at once I saw something
that roused me in good earnest—a black shining thing, like a long strip
of velvet, came gliding into the tent. I knew it directly for one of the
deadliest snakes in Australia. The next moment I heard the rustle of
its coils up the tent-pole to which my hammock was slung, and then I
saw its flat head and black beady eyes hanging over me, and looking right
down into my face to see if I were dead or not. I suppose it thought I
was, for the next minute it slid down over my face, and to and fro along
the hammock, till at last it went to the other pole, and there it glided
off, and I saw no more of it. Anybody watching me then would have
called me a brave fellow; but I dare say it's not the first time that a man
has been thought brave because he couldn't run away!

"I don't know how long it was after that—it may have been an hour,
or a day, or a week, for all I could tell—that a shadow fell across my
face, and I heard a voice calling out, 'Holloa, mate! can you give us a
firestick? I've let my fire go out!' With the sound of that voice all my
love of life came back again, and I gathered up my strength to try and
speak.

"Seeing me lying there so white and still, the fellow must have thought
me dead; and for a moment—the bitterest moment I ever had—I thought

he was going to turn and go out again; but, although I couldn't speak, I managed just to move my eyelids, and he saw it. He said nothing, but raised my head on his arm, and took out his flask to pour some rum into my mouth; and then I knew that I was saved, and with the shock of the reaction I fainted in right earnest."

Here my strange companion suddenly ceased, and, rising from his chair, said to me, ' You've had your story, stranger, and now I'm going to bid you good night; for I haven't spoke of this business since it befell me, and it rather upsets me thinking of it. You tell me you're off early to-morrow morning, so it's a hundred to one if we ever meet again; but, in any case, I wish you success in your travels, and may you end better than *I* have done!"

Then grasping my hand with a force that made it tingle to the wrist, he departed.

His parting words were true, for we have never met since that night; but should these lines ever meet his eye, it may gratify him to know there is at least *one* man in the world who fully believes his story, even though it be (as he styled it) "the strangest adventure of all."

A RECOVERED MANUSCRIPT.

A very important discovery is announced by Professor Benfey, in the *Allgemeine Zeitung*. Many of our readers are aware that there exists an Indian fable-book called " *Panchatantra*," ("the five books,") which in itself is an extract of a larger Sanscrit work, dating from about the sixth century of our era, treating, in from twelve to fourteen chapters, political questions in the guise of "animal fables." This larger work, however, owing to this very extract, or rather selection in an enlarged form, which had become extremely popular in India, not only fell into oblivion on its native soil, but disappeared bodily. Previous to its remodeling, however, this original had found its way into Persia, and was there translated into Pehlvi, and this version was also lost. Not, however, before it had again been translated into Arabic, and out of this last rendering have flowed the innumerable mediæval and modern eastern and western translations, by which this so-called book of "Kalila and Dimna" has become familiar in European literature. Besides this Pehlvi version, however, there had existed, according to a Nestorian writer of the thirteenth century, another in Syriac, also done from the original Sanscrit work, and also dating from the sixth century. But no trace of book that you'd never give me credit for; but in a book this story I'm going to tell you would be impossible; and it's just *because* it seems impossible that it is true."

"So says Byron," interrupted I, speaking lightly, in order to dissipate the effect involuntarily produced upon me by the terrible emphasis of the man's tone and manner.

"I've read Byron too," he rejoined, "though you mayn't think it. That description of the sunset in Greece was always a favorite bit of mine.

"But I must get to my story. You remember how those two fellows robbed my tent, and how I fired all the six barrels of my revolver into them as they ran off? Well, it was just after that job that I shifted my tent away from the rest, thinking I'd be more comfortable by myself for a bit. You'll say this was rather venturesome, after I'd been robbed once already; but then, you see, these beauties that I fired at thought they'd fairly cleaned me out. Nobody knew that I'd got a lot more buried under a big gum tree some two hundred yards off; so the whole camp thought I was dry, and you may be sure I did not undeceive them. Well, I moved my tent up to the tree where the gold was, and there I stayed; but I still stuck to my digging, to make up for what I'd lost. I got a middling lot of dust every day, but I took care to let nobody see more of it than I could help; so folks got to think I was down on my luck, and left off minding about me at all.

"One night I'd been working pretty late, and got chilled right through; and, though I rolled my blanket well round me after turning into my hammock, I couldn't get warm anyhow; and so I shivered away till I fell asleep. Then I fell to dreaming that I was in a trance, like some man I once read about in America, and that they thought me dead, and were going to bury me. I tried my hardest to move, or scream out, or something, but no good; and I heard the coffin-lid slap to, and the first spadefull of earth fall on it, and then I awoke.

"It was a fine bright morning, and through the opening of the tent I could see the sun shining, and hear the picks and cradles getting to work as usual. But my dream wasn't *all* fancy, for I felt as if I were bound down and couldn't move an inch; and yet it wasn't quite that either; it was more as if I had no substance left, but was all air and shadow. If ever a living man felt like a ghost, I did then.

"Well, I didn't think of being frightened just at first; I felt more put out and foolish, like a man who's had a tumble, or got splashed all over by a cart. It seemed so queer for a great strong fellow like me to be laid by the heels that way, and at first the thought of it almost made me laugh; so there I lay like a log for ever so long, listening to all the noises it had ever been found; and, indeed, the Nestorians' account of it was considered, by no less an authority than Silvestre de Sacy, to be based on some mistake, and utterly groundless. Yet who shall say what these latter days of ours will not bring to light? This Syriac version, the oldest manuscript, embracing the whole contents of the lost original Sanscrit work, has suddenly turned up, and the circumstances of its recovery form not the least interesting part of the story. The very first inkling of its existence was brought by a Syrian archdeacon from Ooroomiya, named Jochanan bar Babish, who, in May, 1866, spent some time in the library at Munster, for the purpose of collecting manuscripts. He told Professor Bickell there, that some time ago certain Chaldee priests, who had stayed with the Thomas Christians in India, had brought back copies of the book in question, and had made a present of one to the Catholic patriarch of Elkosh, (near Mossul.) The story seemed—more especially as emanating from that not very trustworthy scource—rather apocryphal, and no further steps were taken to ascertain its truth. Two years afterwards, however, Professor Benfey was informed by Bickell, that the very patriarch to whom the copy was said to have been presented was attending the Vatican Council at Rome. Both he and another Chaldee ecclesiastic, temporarily in Rome, were at once communicated with, and their answer, dated about this time last year, proved the archdeacon's news to be fallacious, but at the same time made the existence of a like manuscript at Mardin most probable. Benfey, upon this, addressed himself without further delay to Dr. Socin, from Basle, then traveling in Asia. Socin, on his part, did not hesitate to act on the hint, though, as he said, with but little hopes.

In a letter announcing the discovery, he writes to Benfey that there was, as he knew by experience, little credence to be given to the boastings of the Oriental Christians regarding the literary treasures in their possession. In the course of his prolonged journey through the " Christian Mountains," the Tur el Abedin, he had visited many monasteries little known before, but he hardly ever saw anything but Bibles. Moreover, all books were watched over with fanatical eyes, and there was nothing to be got by purchase; possibly bribery might do something, but even that only under exceptional circumstances. He went, however, to Mardin. The only likely place he could think of there was the library of the Jacobite monastery, Der ez Zaferan, five and a half leagues from Mardin, in the mountains. After some difficulties he obtained access to it, but having examined its whole stock of about four hundred very commonplace books, he returned disappointed to Mardin, where again he made the most diligent inquiries, without any result. At last one day he " took his heart into both hands," and went boldly into the Chaldee monastery itself; a step all the more hazardous, as he happened to live in the American mission-house, and the Christians of the different sects of that locality were not on the very best terms. More especially did the Catholics of the monastery hate these Protestant missionaries. Luckily, Dr. Socin's servant was a Catholic, and, having given his master a most unexceptionable character, the latter was admitted into the library. Again nothing but prayer-books and Bibles at first, until Socin asked point-blank whether they had any fable books. "Yes, there was one," was the instant answer. A volume was brought, and on being opened, at once proved to be the precious MS. There stood the title, "Lalilag v Damnag," in red letters, as large as life, showing further, by the final "g," that it was not a translation from the Arabic, as had been suspected. Dr. Socin, of course, "dissembled," and the worthy father had not the faintest inkling that that was the work for which he had been specially asked under its title; which says but little for the father's scholarship. A few days after, "a worthy man" was dispatched by our savant to "borrow" the volume. Asked whether it was not rather the Frengi, "the Prot" (Protestant) who had sent him, he strenuously denied this, and obtained the prize. Once holding it in his possession, Dr. Socin grew bolder, and sent messages to the monastery to inquire for the price at which they would part with it. An indignant reply and strong suspicions were the result; but Socin had already handed the work over to copyists, and shortly afterwards received, "*post tot discrimina rerum,*" the copy in question safely at Aleppo. He then dispatched it to Professor Benfey, who, together with Dr. Hoffman and Professor Bickell, is now engaged in editing it. The only question yet to be solved is, whether this translation flowed directly from the Indian original or from the Pehlvi rendering. Anyhow, it is the oldest version in existence of the irretrievably lost Indian original, and is, as such, if for no other reason, one of the most precious documents extant.

THE SMITTEN BUILDER.—The old lectures used to say: "The vail of the temple is rent, *the builder is smitten,* and we are raised from the tomb of transgression." Hutchinson, and after him Oliver, apply the expression—"The smitten builder"— to the crucified Saviour, and define it as a symbol of His divine mediation; but the general interpretation of the symbol is, that it refers to death as the necessary precursor of immortality. In this sense, the *smitten builder* presents, like every other part of the third degree, the symbolic instruction of Eternal Life.

Editor's Easy Chair.

Every editor is supposed necessarily to have an Easy Chair, as a part of the paraphernalia of his office, seated in which, in the quietude of retirement, he thinks of many little things which may be pleasant to his readers, and gives utterance to his thoughts in brief and random passages, the value of which he complacently hopes is not always to be appreciated by their size; for brevity, it will be remembered, is the soul of wit. The Masonic Editor is not willing to be debarred of any of the privileges or enjoyments in which his *profane* contemporaries are wont to delight. He, too, therefore, assumes the Easy Chair, and, comfortably seated within its capacious limits, gives free scope to multifarious thought. And the result will be, in the NATIONAL FREEMASON at least, that a few of its pages will be devoted monthly to a reception and a record of many scraps of Masonic literature, antiquities, and symbolism, too brief for leading articles, but yet, perhaps, containing some hints and suggestions, some facts and anecdotes, which may afford entertainment to its readers, and not utterly valueless as contributions to the fund of general knowledge. Their brevity will at least have this advantage—that it will secure them from being tedious, and that if any of them prove to be failures, the reader will have lost less time in their perusal than if he had spent an hour on a heavier, but equally worthless article. These little paragraphs will constitute the small currency of our magazine; each, we hope, will be worth something, and that, in the aggregate, they will take an appreciable value. At least, we will spare nothing to make the notes which issue from our Easy Chair acceptable and profitable to our patrons.

THE OLDEST MASON.—

"The oldest Mason," like the "oldest inhabitant," has begun to assume the appearance of a myth. The claim has been so often made, and been so often superseded by a superior claim, that we begin to doubt whether such a being as "the oldest Mason in the United States" really exists or ever has existed. The latest of these mythical stories, which is now going the rounds of the newspapers, is to the effect that the Methuselah of the Brotherhood has at last been positively found in the person of a venerable gentleman, who has attained the ripe age of one hundred and fifteen years, has been a member of the Order the long period of ninety-seven years, and is said to have been initiated on the frontiers of Persia, when eighteen years of age. This aged person is a Russian, and resides in Alaska, where he will, no doubt, soon be *interviewed.* It is due to the energy of ex-Secretary Seward that this venerable Mason is now a resident of the United States. This acquisition may be considered as a partial atonement by Mr. Seward for the part taken by him against the Institution in the old anti-masonic times.

A better authenticated story comes to us in the account of the death, on the 24th of August last, in Summit County, Ohio, of Bro. Rial McArthur, who is claimed to have been the oldest Mason in the State, and the last surviving member of the first Grand Lodge of Ohio. Bro. McArthur was eighty-eight years of age at the time of his death. Due honor was paid to his memory, by the attendance at his funeral of a large number of the Brotherhood.

But the championship must be awarded to the Hon. John Prentiss, of Keene, New Hampshire, who is now ninety-three years of age. He received his degrees in 1807, and has, therefore, been a Mason for sixty-four years. What a diary he could write of the doings of the Craft during those eventful years of a Masonic life.

CONSECRATED BREAD.—

Consecrated bread and wine, that is to say, bread and wine used, not simply for food, but made sacred by the purpose of symbolizing a bond of brotherhood, and the eating and drinking of which is sometimes called the "Communion of the Brethren," is found in some of the higher degrees, such as the Order of High Priesthood in the American Rite, and the Rose Croix of the French and Scotch Rite.

It was in ancient times a custom religiously observed, that those who sacrificed to the gods should unite in partaking of a part of the food that had been offered. And in the Jewish Church it was strictly commanded that the sacrificers should "eat before the Lord," and unite in a feast of joy on the occasion of their offerings. By this common partaking of that which had been consecrated to a sacred purpose, those who partook of the feast seemed to give an evidence and attestation of the sincerity with which they made the offering, while the feast itself was, as it were, the renewal of the covenant of friendship between the parties.

GRAND ENCAMPMENT AND GENERAL GRAND CHAPTER OF THE UNITED STATES.—

While we are writing, preparations are being made in various sections of the United States for the Triennial Convocations of the General Grand Royal Arch Chapter and the Grand Encampment of Knights Templars of the United States, to occur in September, 1871, at Baltimore. There is promise of an interesting assemblage. The indications are that several thousand Templars and Royal Arch Masons will be present—certainly many more than have ever attended any previous Conventions. Topics of no common interest will be brought forward for discussion, and the best talent of the Institution will find ample room for display in their settlement. When this number shall appear, the two bodies will probably be in session, and we have made arrangements to give in our next an adequate report of the proceedings.

HONORS JUSTLY PAID.—

Lafayette Royal Arch Chapter, No. 5, of the City of Washington, at a recent Convocation, elected as life members the Marquis of Ripon, (late Earl de Grey,) Grand Principal Z of the Grand Chapter of England; Lord Tenterden, Principal Z of the Chapter of Iris, London; Sir John A. Macdonald, of the Grand Chapter of Canada; and William James Hughan, the distinguished Masonic historian. Life membership in Lafayette Chapter may be considered of some value, as the Chapter is very chary in the bestowal of that honor, it having been hitherto granted to only three persons: Bros. Albert Pike, Albert G. Mackey, and Ben Perley Poore.

RELICS.—

Solomon's Lodge, No. 1, of Savannah, Georgia, has in its possession an oak chair made from the tree under which General Oglethorpe held the first Masonic lodge at Sunbury, Georgia, and the Bible which was used on that occasion, in the year 1733.

ANSWERS TO CORRESPONDENTS.—

In our future numbers we shall devote one or more pages, as circumstances may require, to replies to the numerous letters seeking information on subjects of Masonic history, usage, and jurisprudence. As the letters of this nature which we receive during the month are not very few in number, we shall, by this public method of reply, give greater extension to the information sought, and save ourselves, in many cases, from the necessity of replying to the same question proposed by different correspondents.

𝔅𝔬𝔬𝔨 𝔑𝔬𝔱𝔦𝔠𝔢𝔰.

WORKS OF B. B. FRENCH.

The Grand Royal Arch Chapter of the District of Columbia has appointed a committee to prepare for publication the Masonic and Poetical Works of its late Grand High Priest, Companion Benjamin Brown French. The committee consists of E. Companions John Edwin Mason, Grand Principal Sojourner; Joseph Daniels, Deputy Grand High Priest; and Joseph T. Brown, Past High Priest. This committee has been at work for several months among the vast accumulations of manuscript left by our beloved brother, and find that many of his earlier and more precious articles upon Masonry have not been preserved, and are not to be found among his papers. Desiring to publish a full narrative of his Masonic career, as well as his most valuable Masonic orations, addresses, and poems, the committee are obliged to make a direct appeal to his old friends in Masonry, who may be in possession of any of his orations, addresses, or poems, as well as important contributions from his pen, to forward them to Washington at once. If the owners wish to preserve the copy sent, a faithful pledge of honor is given by the committee, that whatever is sent will be copied and returned to the owner immediately. We beg all Masons to comply with this request, and we shall then have a fine contribution to Masonic literature, when the works of this distinguished Mason are published.

The chairman of the committee will attend to this personally, so that all printed or written matter can be forwarded by mail or express to Dr. John Edwin Mason, Washington, D. C.

HUGHAN'S HISTORY OF FREEMASONRY IN YORK.

We are indebted to the courtesy of Bro. Robert Macoy for a copy of this work, which has been reprinted with great accuracy and beauty by the Masonic Publishing Company. Every one who has paid any attention to Masonic literature must be familiar with the labors of Bro. Hughan in the field of early English Masonic history, and especially his searching analysis of what has been recently called the 1717 theory. If we are not prepared to subscribe to all the opinions of Bro. Hughan, we do not fail to appreciate his profound researches, and his fair and impartial, if not always conclusive, arguments. The present work, which contains in its second part a valuable collection of the hitherto "Unpublished Records of the Craft," came to hand on the eve of our publication, and too late therefore for a more extended notice; but we propose in a future number to review at length the views, the arguments, and the conclusions of our learned brother, as advanced in his early history of Masonry in England.

NATIONAL MASONIC WELCOME TO THE GRAND MASTER OF MASONS OF ENGLAND.

The committee who had in charge the conduct of the late festival, given by the Grand Lodge and the Masons of the District of Columbia to the Earl de Grey, Grand Master of the Masons of England, have appropriately concluded their arduous labors by the publication of a work under this title. It is a book of 79 pages, neatly and artistically printed by McGILL & WITHEROW, of this city. It contains the preliminary correspondence of the Earl de Grey with the committee, an account of the ceremonies on the occasion of the reception and the banquet, the letters of those distinguished Masons who were invited, but could not attend, and the speeches of those who were present. It is, on the whole, a production well worth reading, for the delightful sentiments and utterances which are scattered through its pages, and well worth preserving as a record of what may justly be considered an important event in American Masonic history.

We will not go so far as to suppose that this friendly intercourse of English and American Masons, and this cordial interchange of sentiments of brotherly love, has had or could have any effect upon the political relations existing between the two countries. Anglo-Saxon Masonry takes no part in the battle of politics. Whatever accusations have been made, falsely or not, against the Freemasons of Continental Europe, and their descendants in the Mexican and South American Lodges, even Barruel, the most implacable of the enemies of the Institution, was compelled, by a sense of truth, to exempt the English Lodges from his sweeping charges of political interference. No such object was sought to be accomplished by the American Masons in this demonstration of respect to their English brethren. But Masonry is one of the elements of civilization, and one of the results of civilization is the union in kindlier bonds of the nations of the earth; and the social effect that has been and will continue to be produced by this commingling of hearts and hands is of the most cheering character.

It cannot be denied that there has been, as a consequence of certain events which occurred during the late civil war, an unpleasant feeling between the two countries, which has not always been smothered by the press of either. The press, indeed, has vast influence in directing and controlling the national sentiment; and a recent American journalist has emphatically but justly said:

"All the Washington treaties that may be signed and sealed for the next half century, will not avail to bring about a cordial amity between England and America, unless these parchments are aided by the good will of the press on both sides."

There is unfortunately too much truth in the charge of "cousinly spite" made by this writer, as exhibited in "the general tone of the English press," with very few exceptions.

But Freemasonry has its press as well as its influence, and we are proud as Masons to acknowledge that this "cousinly spite" has never found its way into the English Masonic press.

People, whether Masons or not, will have to learn that two treaties were signed at Washington—one by the Joint High Commission in the Department of State, and the other by the Masons of England and America in the Masonic Temple. The first may or may not be successful in settling the political difficulties which have existed between the two countries. On this question politicians differ, and this is not the place to enter upon its discussion. But we are sure that the second is already producing the happiest results, in securing a warmer and kindlier social feeling between the peoples of the two countries. We need no better evidence of this than the following extract from an editorial in the London Freemason, the leading organ of the English Craft, which we gladly transfer to our pages:

"We feel satisfied that the English Craft will treasure within its heart of hearts the many kind and beautiful expressions of fraternity and fellowship on the part of our American brethren, which we have now placed on record. May the union of the two nations be perpetual; may their march be ever in the van of progress and civilization; their victories those of peace; their rivalry but a friendly emulation in the arts that tend to increase the comfort and happiness of the human race. That our ancient science of Freemasonry *can* contribute to so blissful a result none but the veriest skeptic can doubt, and that it *will*, may be fairly predicted from the cordial relations which are now established between British and American Craftsmen."

𝕿𝖎𝖉𝖎𝖓𝖌𝖘 𝖋𝖗𝖔𝖒 𝖙𝖍𝖊 𝕮𝖗𝖆𝖋𝖙.

FREEMASONRY AT HOME AND ABROAD.

PREPARED FOR MACKEY'S NATIONAL FREEMASON.

BY BRO. WILLIAM R. SINGLETON.

ALABAMA.—

The fiftieth Annual Communication of the Grand Lodge of Alabama was held at Montgomery, December 5, 1870; M. W. Wm. P. Chilton, Grand Master, and R. W. Daniel Sayre, Grand Secretary; 233 Lodges were represented, 374 in the jurisdiction, 104 Lodges suspended, 270 on the register; initiations 989, Master Masons 10,985. The Grand Master's address, of sixteen pages, is devoted to the interests of the Craft and a report of his own official acts. The transactions of the Grand Lodge were characterized by promptness and business tact. The Craft is in a very flourishing condition in that jurisdiction.

ARKANSAS.—

The thirty-second Annual Communication was held at Little Rock, November 21, 1870; M. W. Wm. D. Blocker, Grand Master, and R. W. L. E. Barber, Grand Secretary; 113 Lodges were represented; number of Lodges, 234; initiations, 1,127; Master Masons, 9,324. The Grand Master's address occupies eighteen pages of the proceedings, in which he reviews the transactions of the year, and reports in detail, under their appropriate heads, his various official acts. Two Masters of Lodges had been impeached during the year: One case he dismissed without suspension; in the other he suspended the Master, and directed him to appear before the Grand Lodge for trial. The report on foreign correspondence is by Bro. O. C. Gray, who reviews the proceedings of thirty-nine Grand Lodges in 186 pages.

CALIFORNIA.—

The twenty-first Annual Communication was held at San Francisco, October 11, 1870; M. W. Leonidas E. Pratt, Grand Master, and R. W. Alex. Gurdon Abell, Grand Secretary; 148 Lodges were represented, and 4 Lodges under dispensation; number of Lodges, 175; initiations, 877; Master Masons, 9,528. Fourteen pages of the proceedings are devoted to the address of the Grand Master, which is a very able document, and in which he presents to his brethren much good and wholesome advice, as well as detailing the official transactions of his office and the Craft in general. The report on foreign correspondence is by Bro. Wm. H. Hill, who reviews the proceedings of thirty-eight American and twelve foreign Grand Lodges, and fills 81 pages.

COLORADO.—

The tenth Annual Communication was held at Central City, September 27, 28, 1870; M. W Henry M. Teller, Grand Master, and R. W. Ed. C. Parmelee, Grand Secretary; 9 Lodges represented; number of Lodges, 15; initiations, 118; Master Masons, 854. The M. W. Grand Master delivered an address of only four pages, which was as good as it was short, and so good that we wished there "was more of it," like Mr. Weller's love letter. The report on foreign correspondence is by Bro. L. N. Greenleaf, and reviews the proceedings of thirty-eight Grand Lodges.

CONNECTICUT.—

The eighty-third Annual Communication was held at New Haven, May 10, 1870; M. W. Asa Smith, Grand Master, and R. W. James K. Wheeler, Grand Secretary; 103 Lodges were represented; initiations, 872; Master Masons, 13,072. The address of the Grand Master, like the preceding one, occupies only four pages, and is devoted to the affairs of his office. He mentions having represented his Grand Lodge at the banquet given in this city to the Grand Master of England, last April, by the Grand Lodge of the District of Columbia. The report on foreign correspondence is by Bro. Wheeler, Grand Secretary; forty-five Grand Lodges are reviewed. M. W. James L. Gould was elected Grand Master, and Bro. Wheeler re-elected Grand Secretary.

FLORIDA.—

The forty-first Annual Communication was held in the city of Jacksonville, commencing February 14, 1871; M. W. Samuel Pasco, Grand Master, and R. W. DeWitt C. Dawkins, Grand Secretary; 47 Lodges made returns, and 30 represented; number of Lodges, 54. The Grand Master's address is characterized by sound sense and good reasoning, and much of it is devoted to the discussion of Masonic principles, as well as mere business matters. The report on foreign correspondence is by Bro. Grand Secretary Dawkins, who reviews the proceedings of forty-five Grand Lodges, and gives a summary of all their decisions on general topics, without following the usual formula. Bro. Samuel Pasco and Bro. Dawkins were re-elected.

GEORGIA.—

The Annual Communication was held at Macon, October 25, 1870; M. W. Samuel Lawrence, Grand Master, and R. W. J. Emmett Blackshear, Grand Secretary; 198 Lodges were represented; number of Lodges, 268; initiations, 906; Master Masons, 13,921. The Grand Master's address fills eleven pages of the proceedings, in which he reviews all of his official acts in the form of a diary, giving the date of each event consecutively. In most of his visitations to Lodges he had delivered addresses upon moral and Masonic subjects. The report on foreign correspondence is by Bro. Grand Secretary Blackshear; it occupies eighty pages, and is a review of a mass of matter, as he says, "measuring about two feet in height, and numbering over ten thousand pages." The Grand Master, Bro. Lawrence, and Grand Secretary, Bro. Blackshear, were re-elected.

IDAHO.—

The third Annual Communication was held at Boise City, October 3, 1870; R. W. Samuel B. Connelly, Deputy Grand Master, presiding, in the absence of the Grand Master; Bro. H. E. Prickett, Grand Secretary, *pro tem.*; 8 Lodges were represented; the number of Lodges, 8; initiations, 39; Master Masons, 288. The annual address was by Bro. Connelly, which was very brief, occupying but a few lines over a page of the proceedings. The above officers were elected to fill the stations of Grand Master and Grand Secretary. No report on foreign correspondence.

ILLINOIS.—

The thirtieth Annual Communication was held at Chicago, October 4, 1870; M. W. Harmon G. Reynolds, Grand Master, and R. W. Orlin H. Miner, Grand Secretary; 530 Lodges were represented; number of Lodges, 630; initiations, 3,498; Master Masons, 36,250. Twenty pages of the proceedings are filled with the address of the Grand Master, who ably discusses the various topics, both particular and general, which demand his attention. The vast interests of that large and flourishing jurisdiction seem to demand a large share of the Grand Master's work. The report of the committee on foreign correspondence is signed by all the members, and only fills twenty-six pages. R. W. Bro. DeWitt C. Cregier was elected Grand Master, and R. W. Orlin H. Miner re-elected Grand Secretary.

INDIANA.—

The fifty-fourth Annual Communication was held at Indianapolis, May 23, 1871; M. W. Martin H. Rice, Grand Master, and R. W. John M. Bramwell, Grand Secretary; 406 Lodges were represented; number of Lodges, 419; initiations, 2,241; Master Masons, 22,333. The address of the Grand Master is mostly devoted to the affairs of his official station. Six pages of the proceedings are occupied by it. He contrasts the first organization, in October, 1818, with five Lodges to constitute it, and in 1871, with 420 Lodges then on the register. The report on foreign correspondence is by Bro. Thomas R. Austin, chairman. Forty-five pages are given to a review of the proceedings of forty-six Grand Lodges. An admirable tabular statement is given, showing the exact statistics of the Order in the United States, with the names of Grand Masters, Grand Secretaries, and chairmen of committees on foreign correspondence. The officers above named were re-elected as Grand Master and Grand Secretary.

IOWA.—

The twenty-seventh Annual Communication was held at Davenport, June 7, 1870. The session continued three days. 139 Lodges were represented; number of Lodges, 281; initiations, 1,382; Master Masons, 12,458; M. W. Bro. John Scott, Grand Master, and R. W. Bro. Thomas S. Parvin, Grand Secretary. In his address the the Grand Master says, "Prosperity has favored our material interests, and a healthful growth has been exhibited in the applications for dispensation, of which 26 have been granted." The Grand Lodge of Quebec was recognized; Bro. William B. Langridge made the report on foreign correspondence; Rev. Bro. J. P. Sanford delivered a chaste, most instructive, and able discourse; Bro. Scott was re-elected Grand Master, and Bro. Parvin re-elected Grand Secretary.

KANSAS.—

The fifteenth Annual Communication was held in the City of Atchison, October 19, 1870; M. W. John H. Brown, Grand Master, and R. W. E. T. Carr, Grand Secretary; 64 Lodges were represented; number of Lodges, 93; initiations, 525; Master Masons, 3,761. The Grand Master's address, of twenty pages of the printed proceedings, is given to a free discussion of various interesting topics, but mostly to official matters in his jurisdiction. The report on foreign correspondence, by Bro. Grand Secretary Carr, reviews the proceedings of forty-four Grand Lodges. The Grand Master and Grand Secretary were re-elected.

KENTUCKY.—

The seventy-first Annual Communication was begun and held at Louisville, October 17, 1871; M. W. Charles Eginton, Grand Master, and R. W. J. M. S. McCorkle, Grand Secretary; 357 Lodges were represented; number of Lodges, 481; initiations, 1,841; Master Masons, 20,328. The Grand Master's address, occupying twelve pages of the printed proceedings, is an admirable paper, and breathes the right Masonic spirit. He contrasts the five Lodges called to order on the 16th of October, 1800, with the four hundred and eighty-one Lodges now existing in Kentucky. "The increase of members and organizations," he says, " has made no variance; peace, concord, and unity continue." M. W. Charles Eginton was re-elected Grand Master, and R. W. J. M. S. McCorkle, Grand Secretary. The report on foreign correspondence is from the pen of that admirable and ready writer R. W. Bro. McCorkle, Grand Secretary; and, with his usual care and industry, he reviews the proceedings of thirty-seven American and two foreign Grand Lodges.

LOUISIANA.—

The fifty-ninth Annual Communication was held at New Orleans, February 13, 1871, session five days; 85 Lodges were represented; number of Lodges, 148; initiations, 733; Master Masons, 7,307. The Grand Master notices the alarming epidemic which prevailed during the past summer in many parts of the State. He mourns the loss of eight members of the Grand Lodge, and three of the representatives of his Grand Lodge near sister Grand Lodges. He had issued eight dispensations to form new Lodges; made thirteen decisions. M. W. Samuel M. Todd was re-elected Grand Master, and James C. Batchelor re-elected Grand Secretary. The committee on foreign correspondence, in reply to some comments of the committee of Indiana, (1870,) in relation to the difficulties between the Grand Lodge of Louisiana and the Grand Orient of France, refers to the report of 1870, page 129, *et seq.*, for a very full and satisfactory account of the formation of symbolic chambers in the Grand Lodge in 1832, and the succeeding measures, which was compiled from the original records.

MAINE.—

The fifty-second Annual Communication was held at Portland, May 2, 1871; M. W. John H. Lynde, Grand Master, R. W. Ira Berry, Grand Recording Secretary, and R. W. Edward P. Burnham, Grand Corresponding Secretary; 144 subordinate Lodges were represented; 154 on the register; initiations 1,130, Master Masons 14,726. The Grand Master's address occupies nearly twenty pages of the proceedings, and, in a very able manner, treats upon many interesting topics, especially relating to the introduction of Masonry into Maine, and also in connection with the history of the Order in Massachusetts. The report on foreign correspondence, consisting of 100 pages, is by that most admirable reviewer Bro. Josiah H. Drummond. Fifty-two annual communications are reviewed.

MARYLAND.—

The Grand Steward's Lodge held its Quarterly Communications January 5 and April 6, 1871, at which matters of financial business were transacted. April 26, a Special Communication of the Grand Lodge was held, to pay the last tribute of respect to the remains of Past Grand Master Anthony Kimmel. The Semi-Annual Communication was held at Baltimore, May 8 and 9, 1871; M. W. Bro. John B. Latrobe, Grand Master, and R. W. Bro. Jacob H. Medairy, Grand Secretary; 77 Lodges were represented. The Grand Master's address is almost entirely devoted to the financial matters connected with the Grand Lodge enterprises, and in which he seeks to point the way out of their difficulties.

MASSACHUSETTS.—

The volume of proceedings contains the minutes of all the Quarterly Communications during the year—March 9, June 8, September 14; Special, October 5; Annual, December 14; Stated, December 27, 1870. At no period in the history of Masonry has there ever issued from any Grand Lodge so important and interesting a document as this volume from the Grand Lodge of Massachusetts. The addresses of the Grand Master and other officers, the reports of committees, and the information to be obtained on all the subjects under consideration, all render this a book to be preserved by the well-informed Mason. M. W. William Sewall Gardner, Grand Master, and R. W. Solon Thornton, Grand Secretary; both of whom were re-elected at the Annual Communication; 152 Lodges were represented; number of Lodges, 183; initiations, 1,813; Master Masons, 20,253. There is no report on foreign correspondence, but the Grand Master, in his address, gives special mention of the subject, so far as it was necessary.

MICHIGAN.—

The Annual Communication was held at Detroit, January 11, 1871; M. W. A. T. Metcalf, Grand Master, and R. W. James Fenton, Grand Secretary; 258 Lodges represented; number of Lodges, 288; initiations, 1,991; Master Masons, 22,172. The Grand Master's address fills 23 pages of the proceedings, and is an excellent paper, in which he reviews his official acts, and renders an account of his stewardship in a very able manner. Bro. John W. Champlin, Deputy Grand Master, was elected Grand Master, and Bro. Fenton was re-elected Grand Secretary, who made the report on foreign correspondence, and reviews, in 39 pages, the proceedings of 44 Grand Lodges.

MINNESOTA.—

The eighteenth Annual Communication was held at St. Paul, January 10, 1871; M. W. C. W. Nash, Grand Master, and R. W. W. S. Combs, Grand Secretary; 74 subordinate Lodges represented; number of Lodges, 87; initiations, 440; Master Masons, —. The address of the Grand Master occupies 12 pages, and is a very excellent document. The report on foreign correspondence, by Bro. A. T. C. Pierson, of 121 pages, reviews the proceedings of 35 Grand Lodges. Bro. Pierson is one of our best reviewers, and this report evinces his usual tact in the selection of matter for comment and review.

MISSISSIPPI.—

The fifty-third Annual Communication was held at Vicksburg, January 16, 1871; M. W. George R. Fearn, Grand Master, and R. W. J. L. Power, Grand Secretary; 203 Lodges were represented; 69 not represented; number of Lodges, 272; initiations, 1,118; Master Masons, 11,254; number of representatives, 227; number of brethren entitled to seats, 244. Nine pages of the proceedings have the Grand Master's address, devoted mostly to local affairs and the foreign relations of his Grand Lodge. The above-named officers were re-elected Grand Master and Grand Secretary. The report on foreign correspondence is by Bro. A. H. Barkley, for the committee; 90 pages are occupied in the review and extracts from the proceedings of 45 Grand Lodges.

MISSOURI.—

The fiftieth Annual Communication was held in St. Louis, October 10, 1870; M. W. William D. Muir, Grand Master, and R. W. George Frank Gouley, Grand Secretary; 240 Lodges were represented; number of Lodges, 368; initiations, 1,963; Master Masons, 18,493; and we noticed the presence of some of the oldest Masons, Past Grand officers of the jurisdiction—Past Grand Masters Carnegy, Foster, and Ralls, and Grand Treasurer John D. Daggett. The Grand Master's address, of 24 pages, is a masterly state paper. Its arrangement of subjects, regularity, and consecutiveness, are worthy of commendation and imitation. Bro. Thomas E. Garrett was elected Grand Master, and Bro. Gouley re-elected Grand Secretary, who also makes the report on foreign correspondence, which shows his usual ability, in the review of 46 Grand Lodges, and fills 123 pages of closely printed matter.

MONTANA.

The sixth Annual Communication of this mountain State was held at Virginia City, October 31, 1870, and the volume which contains the proceedings far excels all the other pamphlets which reach us from every source; M. W. N. P. Langford, Grand Master, and R. W. Solon Starr, Grand Secretary. The Grand Master's address is very excellent, and, although designed mostly for the brethren of his own jurisdiction, will bear reading by Masons in every section. Bro. Cornelius Hodges was elected Grand Master, and the report on foreign correspondence was prepared by him; number of Lodges represented, 13; number of Lodges, 14; initiations, 42; Master Masons, 541.

NEBRASKA.—

The thirteenth Annual Communication was held at Plattsmouth, June 21, 1870; 21 Lodges were represented; number of Lodges on the register, 48; initiations, 238; Master Masons, 1,993; M. W. Bro. Harry P. Deuel, Grand Master, and R. W. R. W. Furnas, Grand Secretary. Report on foreign correspondence reviews 31 Grand Lodges.

NEVADA.—

The sixth Annual Communication was held in the City of Virginia, September 20, 1870; M. W. George W. Hopkins, Grand Master, and R. W. William A. Van Bokkelen, Grand Secretary; 13 Lodges represented; number of Lodges, 14; initiations, 75; Master Masons, 977. The Grand Master's address is of a reasonable length, and much to the point, on the usual topics of interest to the Craft. The report on foreign correspondence is by Bro. Robert H. Taylor. Forty Grand Lodges are reviewed in 133 pages. It is an admirable paper, and one of the best we have seen, doing justice to each subject, and executed in a fraternal spirit.

NEW HAMPSHIRE.—

The Annual Communication was held May 19, 1870. The Lodges represented were 64; M. W. Alexander W. Winn, Grand Master, and R. W. Horace Chase, Grand Secretary. The Grand Master's address is confined to local matters. The report on foreign correspondence, by Bro. John J. Bell, is on the proceedings of 35 domestic and 5 foreign Grand Bodies. M. W. John R. Holbrook was elected Grand Master and Bro. Abel Hutchins Grand Secretary. Number of Lodges on the register, 71; initiations, 449; Master Masons, 6,373.

NEW JERSEY.—

The eighty-fourth Annual Communication was held at Trenton, January 18 and 19, 1871; M. W. Robert Rusling, Grand Master, and R. W. Joseph H. Hough, Grand Secretary; 101 Lodges were represented; number of Lodges, 118; initiations, 950; Master Masons, 9,161. The Grand Master's address fills 10 pages, is confined to business affairs, and a statement of his official acts. M. W. William E. Pine was elected Grand Master, and Bro. Hough re-elected Grand Secretary. Bro. Hough made the report on foreign correspondence, 101 pages, and reviews 40 Grand Lodges.

NEW YORK.—

The Annual Communication was begun June 6, 1871, at New York City; 631 Lodges were represented; 656 on register; number of initiations, 6,142; Master Masons, 77,079; M. W. John H. Anthon, Grand Master, and R. W. James M. Austin, Grand Secretary. Rev. John G. Webster, Grand Chaplain, delivered an address, full of good things on the general interests of Masonry and Masonic principles, which was followed by the address of the Grand Master, devoted mostly to the business of his official station and the transactions of the Craft. The report on foreign correspondence was by Bro. Enoch P. Breed, who, in a very condensed and exhaustive manner, reviews the proceedings of 39 domestic, 4 Canadian, and 12 foreign Grand Lodges, in 100 pages, giving a summary of decisions appended to each. The Grand Master and Grand Secretary were re-elected.

NORTH CAROLINA.—

The eighty-fourth Annual Communication was held at Raleigh, December 5, 1870; 172 Lodges were represented; 220 being on the register; initiations, 532; Master Masons, 8,763. M. W. Robert B. Vance, Grand Master, and R. W. Donald W. Bain, Grand Secretary. Bro. Charles C. Clark was elected Grand Master, and Bro. Bain re-elected Grand Secretary, who made the report on foreign correspondence, in 175 pages, and reviewed thirty-eight Grand Lodges. A Special Communication was held at Raleigh, January 14, 1871, being the Centennial Anniversary of the formation of that Grand Lodge.

OHIO.—

The sixty-first Annual Communication was held at Springfield, October 18, 1870. It was held three days. 394 Lodges were represented; number of Lodges on the register, 409; initiations, 2,272; Master Masons, 24,087; M. W. Alexander H. Newcomb, Grand Master, and R. W. John D. Caldwell, Grand Secretary, who were re-elected. The Grand Master's address touches upon some subjects which are of general interest, as well as devoting much of it to the local affairs of his jurisdiction. The report on foreign correspondence is brief, and arranged in subjects, not by States.

[*To be continued.*]

———————

A ROYAL MASONIC SPEECH.—The Prince of Wales recently visited the Grand Lodge of Ireland, on the occasion of his installation as Patron of the Order in that Kingdom, when he made the following speech, worthy of preservation, for the truly Masonic sentiments that it contains. The Prince has been the object for some years past of much vituperation by the English press; but, since his initiation into the Order, he seems to be very faithfully doing his duty as a Mason:

"BRETHREN: I have now to thank you heartily and cordially for your fraternal reception, and for the honor you have done me. I beg to assure you of the pleasure I feel at having been invested a Patron of the Freemasons of Ireland. It is a source of considerable satisfaction to me to know, that my visit to this country has afforded this opportunity of meeting you brethren in Lodge, and of interchanging these frank and hearty greetings. It is true that I have not been a Mason very long; still, I will take the liberty of saying that, during the short period that I have been one of yourselves, I may not be considered an unworthy member. I was, as you may be aware, initiated in Sweden, and attended the Grand Orient Lodge of Denmark. Since then I had the honor conferred on me of being made Past Grand Master of England; last year I received the high and distinguished rank of Patron of the Order in Scotland; and last, though not least, I have now been raised to the high position which you have just placed me in—that of being elected a member of this Grand Lodge, and Patron of the Order in Ireland. I again thank you for the marked compliment which you have paid me, and I am very glad, indeed, of being afforded an opportunity of meeting my Irish brethren here in Grand Lodge. I thank you from the bottom of my heart. I know we all know how good and holy a thing Freemasonry is—how excellent are its precepts, how perfect its doctrines! But forgive me, if I remind you that some of our friends outside are not so well acquainted with its merits as we are ourselves; and that a most mistaken idea prevails in some minds that, because we are a secret society, we meet for political purposes, or have a political bias in anything we do. I am delighted, brethren, to have this opportunity of proclaiming what I am satisfied you will agree with me in, namely, that we have as Masons no politics; that the great object of our Order is 'to strengthen the bonds of fraternal affection, and make us live in pure and Christian love with all men;' though a secret, we are not a political body; that our Masonic principles and hopes are essential parts of our attachment to the constitution and our loyalty to the Crown."

www.ingramcontent.com/pod-product-compliance
Lightning Source LLC
Chambersburg PA
CBHW070622290526
45790CB00002B/960